D0742257

ROBERT LOWELL AND *Life Studies*

ROBERT LOWELL AND *Life Studies*

REVISING THE SELF

TERRI WITEK

UNIVERSITY OF MISSOURI PRESS
COLUMBIA AND LONDON

University of Missouri Press, Columbia, Missouri 65201
Printed and bound in the United States of America

5 4 3 2 1 97 96 95 94 93

Library of Congress Cataloging-in-Publication Data

Witek, Terri, 1952–
Robert Lowell and Life studies : revising the self / Terri Witek.
p. cm.
Includes bibliographical references and index.
ISBN 0–8262–0923–8 (alk. paper)
1. Lowell, Robert, 1917–1977. Life studies. 2. Self in literature. I. Title.
PS3523.O89L538 1993 93-27832
811'.54—dc20 CIP

♾™ This paper meets the minimum requirements of the American National Standard for Permanence of Paper for Printed Library Materials, Z39.48, 1984.

An earlier version of the second chapter appeared as "Robert Lowell's Tokens of the Self" in *American Literature* 63 (December 1991).

DESIGNER: KRISTIE LEE
TYPESETTER: CONNELL-ZEKO TYPE & GRAPHICS
PRINTER AND BINDER: THOMSON-SHORE, INC.
TYPEFACES: PALATINO AND ZAPF CHANCERY

For Rusty

Contents

Preface

Of the many fine books of Lowell criticism, several in particular have made my own efforts possible. As its title indicates, Steven Gould Axelrod's *Robert Lowell: Life and Art* is indispensable in its treatment of the problematic relationship between self and self-representation with which Lowell lived and worked. I am indebted to Alan Williamson's *Pity the Monsters: The Political Vision of Robert Lowell,* particularly for its many wonderful readings of the *Life Studies* poems, as well as to Stephen Yenser's *Circle to Circle: The Poetry of Robert Lowell* for its audacious schematic of Lowell's work. I owe a more personal debt to Kit Wallingford, not only for her book, *Robert Lowell's Language of the Self,* which broke new ground in its treatment of Lowell's relation to psychoanalysis, but also for her advice in dealing with Lowell's estate. I am grateful to Elizabeth Hardwick for her lively correspondence, and to Paul Mariani and Donald Justice for conversations about Lowell as he was during the *Life Studies* years. I have had as well the advice of many thoughtful readers, including Dabney Stuart, Phyllis Frus, Mark Jarman, and Michael Kreyling. My most particular debt is to Vereen Bell, whose book, *Robert Lowell: Nihilist as Hero,* first invited me to see the courage of Lowell's difficult vision of the world: Bell offered Lowell's manuscripts and abundant moral support while tactfully leaving me to my own thoughts. I am also grateful for financial support from both Vanderbilt University and Stetson University.

Throughout my discussion I refer to the familiar 1964 edition of *Life Studies and For the Union Dead.* I have also quoted frequently from the unpublished manuscripts, footnoting the appropriate file in the Houghton Library collection. Some of the material has been published in other versions in *Robert Lowell: Collected Prose*, edited by Robert Giroux, and I have noted where those may be found. Where I've retyped Lowell's typescript, I have preserved the poet's often inventive misspellings and have tried to indicate where and how Lowell revised the particular drafts by hand. I have not tried to include all of the handwritten marginalia (lists of rhyming words, for example). I have also not attempted to reproduce those revisions I find simply illegible, though I note their placement in the text. Except where I have indicated otherwise, all ellipsis points are Lowell's own.

ROBERT LOWELL AND *Life Studies*

Introduction

In December of 1973, Robert Lowell sold a collection of his papers to the Houghton Library of Harvard University for the sum of $141,000. Piecing together Lowell's process of revision from these manuscripts is an absorbing and sometimes frustrating task. Carefully catalogued by Patrick Miehe, drafts of Lowell's work are numbered and arranged in separate folders that generally follow the organization of the finished volumes. Within those individual files, however, the numbers do not necessarily indicate a chronology: page 6 may contain penciled-in changes that were incorporated in the typescript of page 5. The exact sequence of Lowell's revisions is therefore uncertain, though intelligent guesswork suggests patterns of revision in some poems where handwritten changes are subsequently converted into typescript, the new version again marked by hand, and the changes incorporated anew. Dating of individual drafts is also uncertain; that most are typed means they are legible but virtually undatable from internal evidence.[1] Another complication is that Lowell sometimes worked both ends of a sheet of paper: a draft for one poem may have another upside down at the other end, and that page will show up in one file and not another, further compounding the problem of sequence.

The manuscripts of Lowell's 1959 volume *Life Studies* offer an especially complex problem of analysis because they include

1. This legibility does not extend to Lowell's handwritten revisions. Lowell habitually used all capital letters and rapid block printing to indicate changes, and since he seldom closed these printed letters, and often did not extend their tails or legs very far, many letters resemble each other.

much of the poet's over two hundred pages of autobiographical prose. Robert Giroux's 1987 edition of Lowell's *Collected Prose* has been garnered in part from these manuscripts, and his introduction explains that the origin of Lowell's first forays into prose was a contract negotiated between Lowell and Farrar, Straus and Giroux in 1955. Lowell's own claim that the prose was begun as a kind of therapy while he was recuperating from a breakdown following the death of his mother in 1954 is confirmed by Giroux's report that Lowell had proposed the project himself:

> This was so uncharacteristic of him—he sometimes forgot to sign contracts altogether, or misplaced and lost them, but never before had he proposed one—that I concluded he wanted the legal document to serve as a goad to writing. It was impossible not to connect his sudden interest in writing his autobiography with the shock of his mother's death in Rapallo the previous year.[2]

While the dating of particular chapters in the proposed autobiography is unclear, they were probably compiled over several years: Lowell includes accounts of his time at the Payne-Whitney Clinic as well as descriptions of his stay at McLean's Sanitarium, events that occurred in 1954 and 1957–1958 respectively. At the Houghton Library this "Autobiographical Prose" is grouped in undated folders after the poetry manuscripts, and the titles give an indication of their range: "Antebellum Boston," "I take thee, Bob," "Uncle Cameron," "Grandmother and Mrs. Bowles," "Barnstable," "Dunbarton," "Arthur Winslow," "Pictures of Rock," "Rock," "Washington D.C. 1924," "1929," "My crime wave," "Entering St. Mark's," "The balanced aquarium," "At Payne Whitney," "The raspberry sherbet heart," four untitled files, and one file entitled simply "Miscellaneous worksheets." Giroux describes "Antebellum Boston" and "Near the Unbalanced Aquarium" as "two self-contained and finished sections" of the proposed but uncompleted autobiography, each section bearing the chapter heading chosen by

2. Robert Giroux, Introduction to Robert Lowell, *Collected Prose*, ix.

Lowell.[3] It is not clear, though, that all of the material grouped together as "Autobiographical Prose" in the *Life Studies* section of the manuscripts was intended for the autobiography Lowell proposed in the fifties. At least one section was written later than *Life Studies*: the text of the strange and compelling short story, "The Raspberry Sherbet Heart," uses as background Robert Lowell's family life in New York in the 1960s.[4]

Despite the textual problems, what immediately strikes the reader of Lowell's unpublished manuscripts is the poet's near obsession with revision, and the range of transformations he is willing to work on his material. Robert Lowell was, as evidenced by his drafts, both tinkerer and wrecking crew: he would write in multiple possibilities for single words as well as entertain dramatically different forms, tones, and even themes for an individual poem. The drafts reveal that he also experimented with widely varying dictions. At one point, the drafts of what would become "Memories of West Street and Lepke" include a moron joke. Lowell seems willing to try anything, and the range of his experimentation provides an intriguing subtext to the utter recognizability of his voice. Even in a lugubrious rhymed tribute to Colonel Robert Shaw—a move toward the stark intricacies of "For the Union Dead"—Lowell always sounds like Lowell, and the often unhappy authority of that voice provides the compelling engine that drives both his most famous poems and his most awkward drafts.

In revision Lowell often weighs and reweighs poems so that his troubled voice and its attendant persona increasingly become the poems' central story. In the simplest version of this strategy, the poet will set up a vivid figure ostensibly outside the self (historical figures are particularly attractive to Lowell)

3. The prose grouped together under "Near the Unbalanced Aquarium" in *Collected Prose* is actually compiled from several files in the manuscripts. Note Lowell's revision of "The balanced aquarium" for his final title: it is absolutely typical of Lowell to consider opposite versions of the same word for the same place in a text and have both possibilities make poetic sense.

4. Elizabeth Hardwick identified the sources of this hitherto unknown short story in a letter to the author dated August 1990.

and then rework the poem so the figure is muted and Lowell's persona becomes the poem's most powerful presence. (A neat variation occurs when the poet takes on the persona of the outside figure, something Lowell does more frequently in early poems.) This strategy of a setup followed by a takeover is worked in various ways in the drafts. For example, Lowell sets up tight poetic forms in much the same way that he sets up George Santayana, Lizzie Borden, or his own daughter. Each is used as an alternative possibility of identity that must then be dismantled or, rather, reconstructed as a version of himself.

Lowell's many-layered experimentation with such takeovers in his drafts suggests that despite or perhaps because of the strength of his voice, the poet wants to see whether there is something beyond his own identity and, in a curious way, beyond his power. Feminist Luce Irigaray would argue that such a desire is both generically male and inevitably doomed, for male identity depends on creating a relentless series of others who are not truly "other," but are mirror images of the central ego. Lawrence Kramer applies the Freudian principle behind Irigaray's argument directly to Lowell when he observes that the poet sets "beloved, intimate others in the place of the silent, anonymous Other to whom the poetry of *Life Studies* is really addressed"—that is, Lowell himself.[5] Whatever the final status of Lowell's "others," they certainly seem to have been created in order to be undone. One need only think of the familiar Lowell persona, contemplative and nearly always alone, to see the last stages of the process. What the poet's drafts reveal is the way the scenario is constructed over and over with both daring and a peculiar sense of inevitability.

The manuscripts of *Life Studies*, the volume that marked a turning point both in Lowell's style and in his material, offer the most brilliant example of the way a poet experiments with various possibilities for constructing his identity. In that volume, composed in the decade after his parents' deaths in 1950

5. Luce Irigaray, *Speculum of the Other Woman* (see especially "The Blind Spot of an Old Dream of Symmetry," 13–129); Lawrence Kramer, "Freud and the Skunks: Genre and Language in *Life Studies*," 83.

and 1954, Lowell consciously discards early mentors. By now it is a critical commonplace to note, for example, that in the early *Life Studies* poems the abandoned style seems to be that of Allen Tate as displayed in the high formalism of Lowell's *Lord Weary's Castle*. Lowell appears to need to leave behind all the persuasive voices that once held sway over him, and the structure of the book itself enacts this necessity just as surely as do the drafts of individual poems. Among the early *Life Studies* poems, for example, are a series of tributes to Hart Crane, to George Santayana, and to Ford Madox Ford. The first two-thirds of *Life Studies* is thus hardly a study of "Life" at all, but a series of poems about the powerful dead, grouped around the central figures of Lowell's dead parents. In these earlier poems, Robert Lowell names exemplars even as he supersedes them in the book's forward progress. The wife and daughter of the book's final section are living, troubling presences who are, however regretfully, appropriated within the poems they inhabit. The poet who emerges at the end of *Life Studies* is troubled and alone—paradoxically at the very height of his powers.

Lowell not only bids farewell to his mentors in these poems, he also revises his earlier style by loosening lines, composing autobiographical prose, realigning his prose as poetry. The *Life Studies* material strongly suggests that revision of poetic style, like revisions of mentor figures within individual poems, is a subtle experiment with the poet's own sense of identity. Lawrence Kramer has described *Life Studies* as "an inquiry into the possibility of having a self, and into the self's relationship to language and culture." For Robert Lowell the possibility of having a self is equivalent to the possibility of language. The poet once said of *Life Studies*, "I think I was a professional who was forced, who forced myself, into a revolutionary style in writing *Life Studies*, the biggest change in myself perhaps I ever made or will." In a striking elision, "style" has been made equal to "myself." Katharine Wallingford has drawn our attention to two passages from Lowell's later poetry which indicate that once Lowell made this connection he never dropped it. In "For John Berryman I," Lowell tells his dead friend that "we are words," a comment Wallingford sums up concisely by noting that it "confirms Lowell's sense of the close connection between self and language." In "Our Afterlife II," he explains to Peter Taylor: "I was my interrupted sentence."[6]

Much theory about the construction of the self concurs with the assessment Lowell first made about *Life Studies*, a conclusion learned from years of writing. In a chapter whose name sums up Freudian and post-Freudian semiotic thought, "From Sign to Subject, A Short History," Kaja Silverman follows Freud, Lacan, and Beneveniste in arguing that "subjectivity . . . can only be induced by discourse, by the activation of a signifying system which pre-exists the individual, and which determines his or her cultural identity." The subject is always the subject of speech, and if the subject is one's own identity, then the equation of self and language is unmistakable. Recent theorists of autobiography have astutely applied such theories, making of writing about the self a rich body of literary criticism. Paul Jay cites Paul de Man's explanation of the function and process of representing the self in language: "We assume that life produces its consequences, but can we not suggest, with equal justice, that the autobiographical project may itself produce and determine the life and that whatever the writer does is in fact governed by the technical demands of self-portraiture and thus determined, in all its aspects, by the resources of his medium?" Jay explicates de Man in a way that makes sense of all of Lowell's efforts to rewrite his identity through experimenting with style: "What we always confront in any autobiographical work, he [de Man] argues, is not a series of historical events but a series of efforts to write something. The action proper to autobiography, he insists, is not historical but rhetorical." Jay summarizes the ongoing problem of all autobiographical writing succinctly: ". . . how to use one medium—language—to represent another medium—being."[7]

The equation of style and self that Lowell first articulates in

6. Kramer, "Freud and the Skunks," 97; Lowell, quoted in Stephen Gould Axelrod, *Robert Lowell: Life and Art*, 86; Lowell, *History*, 203; Katharine Wallingford, *Robert Lowell's Language of the Self*, 79; Lowell, *Day by Day*, 23.

7. Kaja Silverman, *The Subject of Semiotics*, 52; Paul de Man, "Autobiography as De-facement," 920; Paul Jay, *Being in the Text: Self-Representation from Wordsworth to Barthes*, 18, 21.

regard to *Life Studies* demonstrates his complete awareness of questions of identity as writing problems, and the fact that he addresses his statements on the subject to other writers indicates that he thought they would understand. The equation becomes particularly poignant in his own case, however, when we consider that for Robert Lowell in the early 1950s, both style and self were in jeopardy. At that time Lowell was recovering simultaneously from a long poetic dry spell and from what had become by then a wearyingly familiar event: a mental breakdown, this time scant months after the death of his mother in 1954. The long recovery and respite, and the year following another serious breakdown in 1957–1958, are the *Life Studies* years, and in them Lowell tried to write his way into a style of poetry that was also a style of being, surely one of the most amazing self-help projects of twentieth-century literary history.

Following Lowell as he wrote and revised across assorted styles in *Life Studies*, my argument tracks its way through various linguistic strategies in order to suggest the possibilities and limitations the poet found in each. Chapter 1 sets the biographical context and argues that Lowell's problematic treatment of possible versions of the self can be seen even in an early poem, "Beyond the Alps," in which Lowell writes out the figure of George Santayana across successive drafts. Chapter 2 examines Lowell's difficult choices for dealing with the family material and those most persuasive of early mentors and models, his parents. It discusses the power-brokering that enabled Lowell to write of his mother's death in prose before he wrote about it in poetry and considers the mother and the father as problematic alternative sources of identity. Chapter 3 assesses Lowell's revisions of autobiographical prose into poetry and theorizes about the consequences for self and style in such reworking, using prose and poetry versions of "Sailing Home from Rapallo" to structure the argument. Chapter 4 shows Lowell reshaping the family story for a new generation as he writes his way into the uncomfortable positions of husband and father in drafts for the late *Life Studies* poems.

While I think *Life Studies* changed Lowell and the way he worked forever, I would argue against the volume as a type of culminating vision. For one thing, Lowell continued to rework his style throughout his life, and the manuscripts testify that he was a chronic reviser of individual poems. Equally notable is the fact that each time he tried a new method he described it as if it were the terrain of a new world: free verse was like "breathing naked air"; prose was "less cut off from life."[8] His enthusiasm for each new way of writing was persuasive and finally familiar, as if he were arguing that each new version of some central story would finally tell it truly. His subsequent disenchantments were also phrased similarly. In each case the new style is insufficient to the material; as he says of the attempt to render experience "photographically" in *Life Studies*, the method was "a limitation."[9] Hence the style of *Life Studies* is by Lowell's standards only one in a series of such breakthroughs, and the self that may be identified with each breakthrough itself becomes endlessly open to revision. The Houghton Library manuscripts offer dramatic evidence of Lowell's sense of the perennially unfinished nature of the project: drafts of *Notebook*, written some twenty years later, include sonnet versions of some of the most famous and most intimate free verse poems of *Life Studies*.

8. "A Conversation with Robert Lowell," interview with Ian Hamilton, 10; "Robert Lowell," interview with Frederick Seidel, 68.

9. "A Conversation with Robert Lowell," interview with Ian Hamilton, 14.

—1—

THE GENESIS OF *LIFE STUDIES*

To see the ways in which Lowell recreates his identity with his poetry, we can turn to a time in which circumstances dictated a change in both. On Valentine's Day, 1954, Charlotte Winslow Lowell died in Rapallo, Italy, after suffering a succession of strokes. By a series of missed connections, her son arrived from the United States an hour after his mother's death. He conferred with Charlotte Lowell's doctor and nurse, made funeral arrangements, and sailed home with his mother's elaborate casket, on which, he later reports, their name was misspelled. After Charlotte Lowell's burial in the family cemetery at Dunbarton, Massachusetts, Robert Lowell, then holding the University of Cincinnati's Chair of Poetry in a January–June appointment, began to show symptoms of what was beginning to be recognizable as another cycle of acute mania. At first, biographer Ian Hamilton reports, Lowell was brisk and almost super-rational as he announced his separation from wife Elizabeth Hardwick, made plans to marry an Italian woman with whom he'd had an intense romantic interlude in 1952, dashed off notes to Ezra Pound, and lectured on the great poet's madness at the university. In early April, Lowell gave a lecture "more or less extolling the Superman ideology"; his subject was Hitler, a preoccupation that had signaled other manic episodes. On April 8 he was committed to a Cincinnati hospital, from which he was moved at the end of April to the Payne-Whitney Clinic in New

York.[1] By mid-June he had suffered a complete breakdown. Lowell recovered with the help of Thorazine, came home to Elizabeth Hardwick on September 15, and then, in the long respite from 1955 through 1957, he wrote and revised most of what was to become *Life Studies*.

This troubled period in the poet's life coincides with a particularly difficult time in his work. Lowell had won the Pulitzer Prize for *Lord Weary's Castle* in 1947, but in 1954 he was writing very few poems. He later remembered this dry spell wryly: "*Life Studies* was windfall. It was after 6 or 7 years ineptitude—a stack of eternity. I remember a cousin proving to someone that I was finished—at only 39! Five messy poems in five years."[2] This period of paucity followed a tumultuous end of a decade: in 1949–1950 alone Lowell had completed his break from first wife Jean Stafford and from Catholicism, married Elizabeth Hardwick, suffered a serious breakdown, undergone his first treatments at Payne-Whitney, and lost his father to a series of heart attacks. Allen Tate later commented on the simultaneity of upheaval in Lowell's private life with this particularly unproductive period as a poet: "As I see Cal over the past twelve years, and no one I think knows him better, three things held him together: the Church, his marriage and his poetry. He gave up the Church; he gave up Jean; and some months ago he virtually gave up poetry."

Tate also surmised that Lowell "had been pushed forward too rapidly as a poet and he had attempted a work beyond his power."[3] If this judgment sounds both protective and patronizing there are particular reasons: Allen Tate had encouraged and particularly influenced Lowell during the *Lord Weary's Castle* period, and Lowell, in moving away from the dense formalism of his early style, was essentially abandoning his early mentor (unsurprisingly, Tate was to dislike and disapprove of most of

1. Ian Hamilton, *Robert Lowell: A Biography*, 207, 209.

2. "A Conversation with Robert Lowell," interview with Ian Hamilton, 12.

3. Hamilton, *Robert Lowell*, 141. The work to which Tate refers is "The Mills of the Kavanaughs," which had appeared in the book of the same name in 1951. The relationship between the two men has been thoroughly documented in William Doreski's *The Years of Our Friendship: Robert Lowell and Allen Tate*.

Life Studies). The poet who had given up the Church, a wife, and the poetry associated with his friend Allen Tate was in flight from those powerful presences that had helped shape his personal and professional identities in the previous decade. The deaths of his parents, especially of his mother, precipitated the problems of identity such a flight entailed, and Lowell was to spend the better part of the next decade sorting out those complexities in *Life Studies*. The task was apparently fearsome. In December of 1954, Lowell had outlined the difficulties of acquiring an appropriate "new style" for his friend Peter Taylor: "I haven't been writing at all until the last two months. . . . It's hell finding a new style or rather finding that your old style won't say any of the things that you want to, and that you can't write it if you try, and yet the petrified flotsam bits of it are always bobbing up where you don't want them."[4]

The poems Lowell managed to write in the early fifties, composed during the time of reassessment, were among the first poems of *Life Studies* (a version of "To Delmore Schwartz" was written even earlier, and is included in the drafts of unpublished poems dated 1938–1946).[5] Begun while Lowell and Hardwick were wintering in Rome, these poems were versions of a poem for Hart Crane and one for George Santayana, who had died in 1952. Other poems from this period, some of them completed after Lowell and Hardwick moved on to Iowa, where the poet was to lecture from February to May of 1953, were "Inauguration Day," "A Mad Negro Soldier Confined at Munich," and "The Banker's Daughter."[6] The manuscripts of these few, mostly hard-won poems document Lowell's ventures away from old patterns and the difficulty of finding a "new style" to say what Lowell suddenly needed to say.

These technical aspects of the dilemma were already familiar to Lowell, although at this time in his career he seemed to feel

4. Hamilton, *Robert Lowell*, 196.

5. Lowell, "Uncollected poems (1938–1946)," file 2157, Houghton Library, Harvard University, Cambridge.

6. Donald Justice remembers that Lowell brought drafts of "The Banker's Daughter" to a poetry workshop that Lowell led at Iowa, a class that also included Philip Levine.

their difficulty more urgently than ever before. Lowell would later say that he was always attracted both to what he called the "highly metrical" and the "highly free," and the struggle caused by this dual attraction figures even in his earliest unpublished verse.[7] What was true at the beginning remained so: even at the end of his career, Lowell was torn between radically different poetic possibilities. The loosened sonnet structures of *Notebook* (1968–1969) and *History* (1973) demonstrate Lowell's continued obsession with the dilemma outlined for Peter Taylor over twenty years earlier.

In the *Life Studies* period, the struggle between opposing forms pits the poet's earlier style as the "highly metrical" (and rigid in other ways) form against which he must rebel. Some familiar devices from the early style remain, and have been refurbished for the new poems, notably the patently assumed persona ("The Banker's Daughter," "A Mad Negro Soldier Confined at Munich") and the use of historical personages as sounding boards for the persona's particular ruminations. But despite these "old style" strategies, in his new poems Lowell was clearly interested in loosening strict rhythm and rhyme schemes, which he seems to have imposed in early drafts and then consciously disrupted. The couplets of "The Banker's Daughter" and "Inauguration Day" are infiltrated by the extra rhyme or the stray unrhymed line, for example, and while almost all the end-words in "For George Santayana" and "Words for Hart Crane" rhyme with another end-word, the pattern is unpredictable. "To Delmore Schwartz" and "Ford Madox Ford" are even more loosely organized, though, like most Lowell poems, they are resonant with internal rhymes.

The further point is that these early *Life Studies* poems seem to be all, at one level, self-conscious exercises in uncoupling the couplet, a form in which Lowell had hammered out much of his early work and to which he remained drawn. Lowell's disruption of the self-imposed order of such basic units of poetic measure indicates the direction all Lowell's experiments in both style and subject matter subsequently were to take. If a poem's

7. "Robert Lowell," interview with Frederick Seidel, 68.

order is a product of tradition, an answer to the authority of the past, then Lowell's strategy in the early *Life Studies* poems is to set up the more highly metrical and hence traditional possibility and then push it toward the tenuous freedom of open forms. In Lowell's case, the procedure suggests that the seductive and dictatorial figure of poesy can be subversively reshaped into an individual poet's own more mutable image and likeness.

If the very first *Life Studies* poems challenge the authority of poetic patterns by setting up technical organizations they then proceed to loosen, the poems that came later demonstrate the poet's increasing boldness about his own presence in the poems. Lowell drops the discreet distance of an obviously assumed persona, for example, or a traditional technique like that of the couplet, and moves closer to the material. In the *Life Studies* poems composed after his mother's death, the speaker seems to be the poet himself, remembering and rearranging his past.

The most dramatic reason for this change in the persona's position is also the most straightforward: the second batch of poems began as autobiographical prose written after Lowell's return home from the 1954 breakdown. When Lowell, fiddling with this autobiographical material, transformed the original prose into poetry he gained airier, more conversational poetic lines and a persona close to the heart of the material. Long after the critical success of *Life Studies*, Lowell was to recall the transformation of style he achieved by this strategy: "My first poems were very highly wrought; they were a young man's poems written during the war. Then, after a while, I wrote a very simple book called *Life Studies*: most of it is almost as simple as prose, in the sense that it could be read aloud and gotten on the first reading. It's about direct experience, and not symbols."[8]

Whether writing prose accomplished all that Lowell claimed for it is problematic and is the subject of future chapters. But Lowell's identification of his *Life Studies* style with "direct expe-

8. "Et in America Ego—the American Poet Robert Lowell Talks to the Novelist V. S. Naipaul about Art, Power, and the Dramatization of the Self," interview with V. S. Naipaul, 304.

rience" rather than "symbols" shows what Lowell was after when he began dismantling the formal structures of his early poems. Making his poetry more like "direct experience" means a move away from those formal structures at which he had become expert, and from the third-person "young man" who had written them. The new style, like the new man, would be impatient with both poetic "symbols" and his own early mentors. In *Life Studies* Lowell sought to depose anything that, at one remove from "experience," kept him from finding new ways to say new things.

Lowell leaves behind old styles and the mentors associated with them, but writers are not the only influential figures he attempts to discard. What these figures have in common is that they are similarly imposing and convincing males (the exception, Lowell's mother, is a telling addition to the list) who offer highly organized and indeed rigid models of identity. Lowell demonstrates an attraction to the "highly metrical" in his choice of such figures similar to his attraction to highly structured poetic forms, in other words. Hitler is the extreme example of the type, but Lowell was fascinated from childhood by Napoleon and other persuasive molders and enforcers of ideas of order, people who worked as imperiously and with as much assurance as did Allen Tate on quite different material. Because Lowell elides questions of style and self so consistently, the pull between what is "highly metrical" and "highly free" can be most clearly demonstrated in his poetry, but it is tempting to interpret some nonlinguistic events in Lowell's life according to what he saw as twin tendencies in his poetic technique. The poet's consistent attraction to military leaders and his status as conscientious objector and later as antiwar activist, for example, can be thought to enact the dual possibilities precisely. This particularly intriguing combination suggests that perhaps such dualities are never as different in kind as they appear to be, that extreme positions are always more interchangeable than anything in the fuzzier middle ground. And certainly the results of Lowell's various attitudes toward the military are eerily similar: Lowell's touting of Hitler was a symptom of the mania that sent him to the hospital, and his stance as conscientious objector and then antiwar demonstrator sent him to jail.

But the make-over Lowell attempts in *Life Studies* is at that time in his life and work balanced toward what he thinks of as freedom—his own personality rather than that of others, his own systems of organization rather than those received from the past. The clearest way to see how Lowell accomplishes what seems to have been both psychically and poetically necessary at the time is to examine an early poem in which the poet visibly pulls back from highly wrought forms and from a mentor who approved of them. The first poem in *Life Studies*, "Beyond the Alps," is justly famous for its portrayal of a solitary persona suspended between cities and, by implication, between modes of being. The *Life Studies* version is only one of several, however: an earlier version had been published in 1953 and then heavily revised for the new book, and another version would appear in Lowell's next volume, *For the Union Dead*. The poem thus publicly attests to Lowell's fascination with revision; more intriguingly, the manuscript material reveals that the poem was at various stages addressed to George Santayana, and sometimes included him as a character.[9] Lowell's process of revision in "Beyond the Alps" suggests that the poet had initially ordered the poem around Santayana's powerful presence. In revision, however, Lowell rebalances structurally in order to write out the figure of this charismatic mentor.

Lowell had visited Santayana frequently in Rome during the winter and spring of 1950–1951, and the two men had also corresponded. The older poet, philosopher, and questioning Catholic is exactly the sort of figure Lowell was always attracted to and would, perhaps, liked to have been: a man who had worked out a relationship with a larger system of order that had not disabled him but rather made him more triumphantly himself, as in the case of Santayana's peculiarly Catholic atheism. Certainly the elder writer showed both sympathy and an acute understanding of Lowell's own troubled response to Catholicism. In a letter dated March 1, 1951, Santayana astutely identifies Lowell's conversion as a type of experimentation in form: "No doubt it was not a refuge for you but an adventure—

9. Lowell, "Beyond the Alps," file 2182, Houghton Library.

a voyage and a love affair in a new dimension." Santayana further demonstrates his astuteness by understanding that Lowell's primary concern is his own identity. In the same letter, he describes Lowell's tendency to organize experience in just this way: "I recognize that your centre, as in Protestant religion, is in yourself, not in the cosmos or history or even society."[10]

With this analysis Santayana suggests the nature of Lowell's perennial dilemma: attracted to powers outside the self, Lowell will always circle back to the "centre." Wooed by "the cosmos or history or even society," Lowell will be drawn to belief in an order outside the self even as he rejects it as obfuscating to "experience." The inherent irony is profound, however, for as astute as Santayana is, and compelling as a possible version of the self, he too belongs to "history" and the "cosmos." As someone outside the "centre" he also must be discarded as somehow dangerous to one's own being.

Lowell's double attraction toward the highly fixed and the highly free assures, however, that the poet does not present himself in "Beyond the Alps" as the virile young hero who overcomes a powerful older male in order to create a triumph for the natural order. Jacques Lacan's idea of the process of becoming a subject has been described in terms that elucidate Lowell's problematic position: the human subject "is not an entity with an identity, but a being created in the fissure of a radical split." Hurtling between Rome and Paris, Lowell's persona in "Beyond the Alps" is, appropriately, an unprepossessing newborn, "blear-eyed" and kicking in his solitary "berth" without a parent in sight. With the gain of his own being comes an overwhelming helplessness, and the sense of loss that will become the predominant tone of *Life Studies*. In the Lacanian scheme of how subjects are born in the text, such loss is always the first side effect of language, for "the subject can only operate within language by constantly repeating" the "moment of fundamental and irreducible division."[11]

As someone who midwives his own rebirth by dividing

10. Lowell, "Letter to Perry Miller," file 1595, Houghton Library.

11. Jacques Lacan, *Feminine Sexuality: Jacques Lacan and the Ecole Freudienne*, ed. Juliet Mitchell and Jacqueline Rose, 5, 31.

himself from what he is so compelled by, Lowell's method is therefore to create entrapments in order to engineer his escape. The poet's desire to flee between the fixed and the free is a flight from what has already been established—powerful role models or already established poetic forms—toward the moment of his birth into language and therefore into being. Later he is able to formulate what the moment looks like in its most basic terms: "I was my interrupted sentence." Laden with characters, uneasy in form, the first poems of *Life Studies* are still far from this spare formulation of what it means to bring oneself into being through words, but the essential process is in place, undergirding Lowell's revisions of perhaps his finest poems. The poem that opens *Life Studies* becomes through its many drafts a complex strategy by which Lowell wills himself away from both the allure of a powerful mentor and the fixity of form despite the attendant, necessary loss.

In the versions of "Beyond the Alps" that include George Santayana, the philosopher's presence is a powerful force, and Lowell's role as a character in his poem is as both disciple and stealthy usurper of his mentor's power. The moral weight of Santayana's presence is clearly attested to in one draft:

BEYOND THE ALPS
for George Santayana
(on the train from Rome to Paris: 1952)

Reading how even the Swiss had thrown the sponge
in once again and Everest was still
unscaled, I watched our Paris pullman lunge
mooning across the fallow Alpine snow;
O bella Roma! Much against my will,
I saw our tri-lingual Roman stewards go
forward on tiptoe banging on their gongs—
I'd left the city of God where it belongs.
There when the skirt-mad Mussolini unfurled
the Eagle of Cæsar, he was one of us
only, pure prose, and less miraculous
than those grand tours that our grand parents made
immortal, while the artist followed trade—
Breezing upon his trust fund through the world.

The crowds at San Pietro screamed *Papa*,
when the vatican made our Mother's *Assunta* dogma.

New England Puritan, was I right to envy
those Italians their bread and circus piety?
Saint Peter's idols, white as death and hope,
turned ultra-violet, when they cheered the Pope.
The lighting washed him a cerulean blue.
Wiping his glasses, he saw as well as we
Morte Americani in full view,
zig-zagging the walls of the *Trastevere*—
No peace on earth! In Rome God is all act.
Here Augustus turned the Republic's bricks to gold.
Stand still, doubt wisely. Ask a hand to hold
God's Mother risen to the realm of fact.

The Holy Father dropped his shaving glass
and listened. His electric razor purred,
his pet canary chirped on his left hand;
the Mother of God ascended like a bird—
the key's were Peter's, he threw away the lock.
Yet who believes this. Who can understand
a God, who breaks the Roman boot on rock,
chastens his chosen with the *coup de grace,*
forgets thee, Sion? Can the evil eye
of Satan, stripped of cloak and dagger, die,
there where the Switzers slope their pikes and push
O pius, through the monstrous human crush?[12]
no heavenly dictator's whiff of grape-
shot rids the Piazza of its lynched and booted shape?

In this closely rhymed, fourteen-line-stanza version of the poem, the philosopher isn't mentioned by name again after the title. Yet Santayana's presence in a position of authority at the poem's beginning (as if it is somehow he who is "Beyond the Alps") seems to ratify the persona's questions and commentary. And, notably, Lowell has dated the train ride "1952," the year of Santayana's death (in the *Life Studies* version the date is "1950, the year Pius XII defined the dogma of Mary's bodily assumption"). This dating makes the poem seem designed as a tribute, perhaps as an elegy, for the philosopher. And while it may seem

12. The *p* of "pius" has been capitalized by hand. The first word in the next line has been crossed out and "what" substituted for it. In the sixth line of this stanza, "Yet" is crossed out and the final *s* in "believes" has been changed to a *d* by hand.

peculiar that Lowell doesn't make Santayana a character in this poem "for" him, the poet subtly connects both himself and Santayana with various other powerful men in this version, suggesting that the world is indeed organized by such virile presences. Lowell and Santayana, linked by the poem's collective pronouns, are joined by Mussolini in a weirdly potent triumvirate. That particular dictator was "like us," only "pure prose"—the phrase suggests again the equality of text and being. Whereas Santayana and Lowell are presumably less "pure" by virtue of being poets, Mussolini is not only unsullied language, but also the most radical extension of a masculine type Lowell finds attractive despite himself. He has elsewhere described it as "the fanatical idealist who brings the world down in ruins through some sort of simplicity of mind."[13]

Here Lowell refers to Ahab, and a part of our heritage he thinks is "a danger for us." Yet the poet is always drawn to such figures, and even George Santayana could be thought of as a version of this type, a powerful intelligence who inadvertently endangers the identity of those around him through the sheer force of his presence. Unsurprisingly, Lowell notes that "the fanatical idealist" is also "in my own personal character," demonstrating his awareness that the type is a disturbing version not only of possible role models, but of himself. If Santayana represents a beneficent version of the type in this draft of "Beyond the Alps," the figure of Mussolini provides a dangerous but appealing reformulation of the problem personality within the text of the poem. He is linked back through time to other strong leaders: to Caesar, and perhaps, in the "whiff of grapeshot" reference, to Napoleon, a frequent presence in Lowell's poems who is often identified with the most powerful and dangerous authority figure of all—Lowell's mother.[14]

These potent figures are matched in this early draft by paler manifestations: Pope Pius XII is an all-too-human man in foggy glasses who may recall Lowell's own father. This pope is no

13. Hamilton, *Robert Lowell*, 327.

14. One source for the "whiff of grapeshot" is *Dictionary of the Napoleonic Wars*, ed. David E. Chandler, 298.

military or intellectual leader but a "Holy Father," or, more familiarly in the native Italian, a "Papa." Like the more political personalities, the pope is shown to be less a cohesive force than a contributor to the peculiar flotsam and jetsam of history. That the human being most ritualistically close to the divine has made the bodily ascension of Mary into dogma is less a transcendent action than a perverse oddity in this draft. Swept by garish blue lights, the pope and his people might be performer and audience in some third-rate entertainment. In Rome, "God is all act." Lowell's declaration is so scathing that he strains credibility when he asks ". . . was I right to envy / those Italians their bread and circus piety?"

Despite his implied criticism of all versions of the powerful male personality, these characters represent the simplicity of mind Lowell not only claimed as part of his own identity, but that he found attractive in such leaders as Mussolini, Caesar, Napoleon, and in various members of his family. Despite his ambivalence toward such figures, by the end of the draft Lowell's persona cries "O Pius," as if he too longs for the guidance of some sort of Holy Father. And, almost surreptitiously, he has stopped addressing Santayana, as if, by the end of the poem, Lowell's persona has found the wherewithal to address Catholicism's pontiff without the bolstering presence of the century's most famous critic of the Faith.

A more plausible reading of this shift in the poem's characters is that the figure to whom the poem is addressed has metamorphosed into someone else by the end of the poem. In this version of "Beyond the Alps" the permutation in the poem's addressee demonstrates how elusive the differences between Lowell's characters are. Mussolini, Caesar, Pius XII, Santayana, even God and Satan, all seem to partake in different measure of the same source of power, divided and refracted in language.

That there are multiple versions of the self, created in division and loss, suggests the fluidity of all fixed forms, even the most persuasive. This fluidity is acted out not only in the characters, but even in the metaphoric substance of this particular draft. Once the canary chirps on the pope's fist, in the very next line Mary has "ascended like a bird," as if she has been transported literally into "the realm of fact." The event is anomalous but hardly transcendent: the Pope holds God's mother in one hand and his shaving equipment in the other.

It would be easy to interpret this world of shifting forms as a diminished one: God may once have been powerful, if incomprehensible, when he "broke the Roman boot," but now a divine event can be contained by the human hand, and Caesar's eagle has become Pius's canary. Lowell is fully aware of the potential for irony implicit in such a discrepancy, and he turns the whole image into an oblique joke: God's representative is not only dim of vision, but sexually incomplete; the "lock" for the papal "key" is gone, and this "Papa" is not the Bride of Christ but a perch for God's mother. The important spiritual relationship seems to be mother-son; the pope is more like a sexless Joseph than like the virile, rocklike "Peter."

Just as the borders between Lowell's characters are yielding, so too the differences between the poem's guiding ideas. If at first to be risen to "the realm of fact" seems less prestigious than to be ascended into heaven, the phrase suggests "pure prose," and we remember that the world that produces canaries and shaving gear is the same fundamentally mysterious source of Caesars and Mussolinis. And if the old God seems hidden, "Satan's malignant eye" is still alive in a city where leaders are lynched and palace guards push their "pikes" into the adoring crowd. The power of such a world has not been diminished but dispersed, loosed from fixed forms, and it has now reappeared in bizarre, relentlessly changing shapes.

"Stand still, doubt wisely," Lowell's persona intones midpoem, as if to arm himself with a piece of Santayana-like advice in this city of dubious alliances and ancient, shifting powers. But while Lowell's persona yearns toward Rome's powerful figures, he knows that his place is literally and philosophically elsewhere: "I'd left the city of God where it belongs." God's mother, the pope, Mussolini, even the transplanted "Switzers" and the "tri-lingual Roman stewards" on the train, all have a clear connection to Rome. So does George Santayana, who, though part "New England Puritan" like Lowell himself, is claimed by the city of both his death and his childhood belief. Much as Lowell wants to recruit Santayana as alter ego and guardian angel, when Lowell's persona leaves Rome, "much against my will," he leaves behind all the poem's summoning figures. He seems compelled to discard those more vivid versions of the self because their very persuasiveness is dangerous. Despite his "will" and his own sense of loss, Lowell's persona makes his own version of flight between forms: he takes the train to Paris.

The mutability of the characters in this early draft is a way for Lowell to talk about the fluid nature of all versions of the self, and to make a claim for the necessity of that fluidity as a strategy to avoid the stultifying power to which he is dangerously drawn. But having written a poem dedicated to the principles of fluid transitions between forms, Lowell seems to see the whole complex web of resonances and associations that result as another kind of trap. He packs up his "blear-eyed ego" and situates himself on a train that has strategically not yet reached Paris, where we may presume he would have to work out the complicated patterns all over again.

Problems of form and the escape from a powerful mentor also provide the subtext of another draft of "Beyond the Alps," originally published in 1953:[15]

Beyond the Alps
(on the train from Rome to Paris)

Reading of how the Swiss have thrown the sponge
In once again and Everest is still
Unscaled, I watch our Paris pullman lunge
Mooning across the fallow Alpine snow;
O bella Roma! It's against my will,
Like the trilingual Roman cooks who go
Forward on tiptoe, banging on their gongs;
I leave the City of God where it belongs.
O gods, when the breast-thumping blimp unfurled
The eagle of Cæsar, he was one of us
Only, pure prose, and less miraculous

15. This poem was originally published in *Kenyon Review* 15 (Summer 1953): 398–401. Lowell tore out the middle two pages from a copy of the journal and revised them by hand; these pages are included with other drafts of "Beyond the Alps" in file 2182, Houghton Library.

Than those grand tours that our grand parents made
Immortal, when the artist followed trade,
While breezing on his trust fund through the world.

O just to dog the crowd! *Papa, Papa,*
Papa, Papa, l'Assunta, Liberta:
New England Puritan, you could only see
A sort of bread and circus piety—
St. Peter's idols, white as death and hope,
Turned ultra-violet, when you cheered the Pope,
Who wiped his glasses, backed against a wall,
And watched the Reds and Blackshirts merge to scrawl
Morte Americani in full view—
The lights had washed them a cerulean blue,
Like Virgins signing on the dotted line:
"No peace on earth." Here saints believe and act;
Bricks turn to gold by fiat. They resign
God's Mother risen to the realm of fact?

The Holy Father drops his looking glass
And listens. His electric razor purrs,
His pet canary chirps on his left hand.
God's in his heaven; Mary's back in furs;
Blackmarket princes liquidate their stock.
O Father, you believe? You understand
Why God, who broke this Roman boot on rock,
Still herds his people to the coup de grace?
Lion of Judah, when the evil eye
Of Satan, cloak and dagger gone, shall die,
There where your Switzers slope their pikes and push,
O Pius, through the monstrous human crush—
Will Cæsar, lynched and booted to blind shape,
Clear the Piazza with a whiff of grape?[16]

I thought of Ovid, for in Cæsar's eyes,
That Tomcat had the number of the Beast.
Where the young Turks are facing the red east,
And the twice-stormed Crimean spit, he cries:
"Rome asked for poets. At her beck and call,
Came Lucan, Tacitus and Juvenal,
The black republicans who tore the teats
And bowels of the mother wolf to bits.
Beneath a psychopath's divining rod,

16. The word *shot* has been handwritten at the end of this line.

Deserts interred the Cæsar-salvaged bog.
Imperial Tiber, O my yellow dog,
Black earth by the Roman sea, I lie
With the boy-crazy daughter of the God,
Il duce Augusto. I shall never die."

Life is for children. At the hospital,
Sister Angelica received my call
Bluely, and put me in your shoes a mile
From nowhere, Santayana. When you died,
True to your boyish shyness of the Bride,
No shock of recognition made her smile.
While the rash Texan Thomist, sent to task
Your old Franciscan wrapper's mongol mask,
Loiters, I see your child's red pencil pass
Bleeding deletions on the proofs you hold
Under your throbbing magnifying glass,
That worn arena, where the whirling sand
And broken-hearted lions lick your hand,
Refined as yellow as a lump of gold.

"Spirit gives life," you say, will letters kill
The calm eccentric, if by heaven's will
He found the Church too good to be believed?
I died, the nuns will tell, *as I lived.*
That's how they rime and riddle what I wrote
Of Christ, whose faith is too pragmatical
To nurse illusion. Jesus wept, when Paul,
Who sowed the winds with dogma, missed the boat.
I preached the truth was what my hand could reach,
And gave the bottomless Evangel soul.
Essence took heart and landscape from my speech.
Dying, I fancied the Blue Sisters pressed
Like geese-girls, hissing, *Rome must give her best.*
Let Curtius in full armor fill the hole![17]

My mountain-climbing train has come to earth.
Tired by the querulous hush-hush of the wheels,
The blear-eyed ego, kicking in my berth,
Lies still, and sees Apollo plant his heels
On terra firma through Aurora's thigh—
Fire-branded socket of the cyclop's eye.

17. The stanza ends at this line in the published version. Lowell has written in another line by hand: "There is no God, and Mary is his mother."

O Machiavellian vision charged with good,
Dog-star of Athens, when the Goddess stood—
Prince, Pope, philosopher and golden bough,
Pure mind and murder at the scything prow—
Minerva, the miscarriage of the brain:
Decipher Europe! Vibrate through my pane . . .
Now Paris, our black classic, breaking up
Like killer kings on an Etruscan cup.

Although Santayana has both a character and a monologue in this version of "Beyond the Alps," the persona has an easier time separating himself from this charismatic figure, largely because Lowell has opted for a type of structural containment of the poem's various characters. Santayana's section comes near the poem's end, and the two penultimate stanzas form part of what will become the separated "For George Santayana." Santayana seems to make his first appearance in the poem earlier, though, demonstrating that characters in this version of "Beyond the Alps" also have a way of merging identities. When Lowell's voice proclaims with what seems to be the Roman crowd: *"Papa, Papa, l'Assunta, Liberta"* the referent is unclear because we have not been directed by the poem's subheading to link the poem to either the pope or the risen Mary. When the "New England Puritan" is addressed in the following line his identity is mysterious; only as the poem unfolds do we note that only Santayana and Robert Lowell himself could be referred to as "New England Puritans." But Lowell has written the lines so that the "Papa," "l'Assunta," and "Liberta" are connected by a colon to this mysterious character: they are made equivalent by the basic grammatical ordering itself. No matter how self-contained these fourteen-line stanzas at first appear (Lowell begins with his own persona, then takes up the pope, Ovid, and Santayana in succession before returning to his own persona at the poem's end) their structure has been infused from the start with a radical sense of the mutability of their characters.

Although these figures are initially treated very unsympathetically (Mussolini, "one of us," is a "breast-thumping blimp"), they are at least subject to human foibles: in this version of "Beyond the Alps," they are confused and beleaguered human beings. Lowell makes these powers less daunting by making them more human, and he is in this context free to be kinder to the failed father figure of the pope, who is at one point "backed against a wall" as if awaiting execution. Lowell's persona addresses him directly, as he did only at the end of the other version, and this time the pope is capable of not only belief, but understanding: "O Father, you believe? You understand why. . . ." This pope is not only "Father" and "Pius," but ironically a "Lion of Judah," and in this version God's business has been reduced from luridly transcendent spectacle to pragmatic commercial venture:

> God's in his heaven; Mary's back in furs.
> Blackmarket princes liquidate their stock.

The assessment is biting, but this description of the Church puts it firmly within the reach of human comprehension, and so within the poet's power. This time around Mary is no mysterious bird-woman perched on the Pope's lathery hand but a well-heeled matron.[18] God seems a human dictator in this version: he doesn't "chasten the chosen" and forget the Jews altogether as in the first quoted version, but "herds his people to the *coup de grace*," an unpalatable function that suggests both Hitler leading the Jews to their deaths and, ironically, God's time-honored position as Good Shepherd. And the stanza's final proposition has been defused by changing its subject: now it is "Cæsar" who may have the power to clear the piazza. The summoning of a historical figure, no matter how godlike, seems more reassuring than that of an unnamed "divine dictator."

The more human the sources of power, the more accessible they are in this version of "Beyond the Alps." Poets themselves are characters with functions in the world as artists and patriots. Ovid is invoked to explain the poets' traditional purpose: the world summons its poets, who then tear her "to bits." The process will occur again and again. The old Roman poets are "black republicans," linked through time to similarly dubbed radical Americans of Civil War history, and by implication to all

18. Or perhaps this is a parodic reference to "Venus in Furs," Leopold von Sacher-Masoch's figure of female domination.

who defy the laws of the land for the land's own good. Lucan, Tacitus, and Juvenal are joined by all poets who question the reigning structures; Santayana and, by extension, Lowell are new formulations of the old posture and purpose.

With the introduction of Ovid, this version of "Beyond the Alps" subtly shifts its characters away from the beleaguered humanness that was their lot in the opening stanzas to offer a new alliance of powerful men, all of them poets. The way they function in the state is almost terrifyingly primal: the old Roman poets "tore the teats and bowels" of the mother wolf, that which nourishes her and by which she nourishes others (this action resonates uncomfortably with Mussolini's buffoonish "breast-thumping"). Rome has summoned her poets to this masochistic ritual; they are, the suggestion is, more vital to her than food. And the imagery is also sexual; the sons savage the mother by her own consent in a type of Oedipal fulfillment. In a related image of sexual purpose, Ovid claims that because he has lain with "the boy-crazy daughter of the God" he "will never die." Here the mysterious primal communion between poets and state serves as a crude but efficient device for gaining immortality.

This touting of savage but morally persuasive poets prepares for the official entrance of Santayana when he is named in the poem's fifth stanza. Unlike Mussolini or the pope, Santayana is initially portrayed very sympathetically as both beset by the world and undeniably noble. This version of "Beyond the Alps" makes of all poets noble humans, and the poem seems to argue that as such they deserve a type of transcendence, a permanence that will ensure their immortality. But Lowell typically engineers a strategy that will allow him to undermine his own assertions. The guiding saint of these noble humans is Ovid, the poet of mutability, and his presence in the poem here seems to dictate the permutations between form that are the subtext of every version of "Beyond the Alps." The position of Santayana, introduced and then sanctioned by the sections that outline the function and importance of poets, is thus set up to undergo a metamorphosis from the beginning. In this version of "Beyond the Alps," Santayana is positioned as a powerful exemplar of ancient moral forces only to have his place in the poem almost immediately usurped by an admiring disciple, Lowell's own problematic persona.

The shift from Pius's section to Santayana's lets Lowell step out of his role as ruminating train traveler and into a new position in the poem; he becomes a poet among poets. In Santayana's section Lowell is so closely allied with the older man that he literally can stand in for him: the Blue Sisters "put me in your shoes." Once Lowell is in Santayana's "shoes," he has access to the philosopher's argument, which we hear from Santayana himself. Lowell has revised the poem to make the point more forcefully. The published text of the poem has been changed by hand so that the general "you say" becomes the specific "you told me." With this important change, Lowell gives himself the privileged role of hearer and transmitter of his mentor's words.

Although Lowell situates his persona in this powerful position, he is careful to maintain his stance as disciple. He cleverly enforces this status by describing another visitor to the hospital in Rome where Santayana was staying, a "rash Texan Thomist" who "loiters" and "tasks" Santayana. Lowell's persona, in contrast, is the good visitor privileged to hear Santayana speak and to watch the old philosopher marking "proofs," a term that suggests both the work they share as writers and the grasp on truth Santayana possesses and Lowell's persona seeks. But for all Lowell's deference, his vision prevails. Although Santayana looks through the "throbbing magnifying glass," Lowell portrays the old man himself trapped within the glass like an aging Daniel in the lions' den, as if to say that the disciple really wields the more encompassing lens. So while Lowell seems careful not to usurp Santayana in this version of "Beyond the Alps," he is actually in the process of dispersing Santayana's power and stationing his persona to take over the poem's central position.

The crucial rebalancing occurs during Santayana's oddly disjointed monologue from beyond the grave. In this stanza Santayana is almost distastefully self-congratulatory, an effect Lowell counters by having the older poet speak of himself at one point in the third person ("He found the church too good to be believed") and at another point by giving the hospital nuns laudatory comments to make on Santayana's behalf ("I died," the nuns will tell you "as I lived"). But the problem with parceling out portions of Santayana's speech is that it disperses Santayana's power as a character in the poem. Even while Lowell places himself as the disciple imbibing the great man's wisdom, he is making loopholes in the stanza that permit other possibilities. Santayana may boast, "Essence took heart and landscape from my speech," but the preternatural geese-girl nuns (this version's image of powerful religious bird-women) get the last line of Santayana's monologue. He "fancies" that they call upon another warrior to fill the void left by Santayana's death: "Let Curtius in full armor fill the hole."[19] This is backhanded praise indeed, as the chorus of nuns by his own invention effectively ejects Santayana from his stronghold and provides the name of a problematic replacement.

This replacement takes the poem away from both Santayana's voice and his person, and allows for a mysterious pronouncement, penciled in by Lowell as if he had acquired the power to speak as Santayana: "There is no God, and Mary is his mother." The statement begins Santayana and ends all Lowell in the revised draft's strangest permutation: it denies God's existence and then, once the name is written, gives him gender and the all-important family relationship. The seriousness of the pronouncement is also undercut by the fact that it sounds like a parody of the Moslem saying, "There is no God but Allah and Mohammed is his prophet." This undercutting is also prototypical Lowell. The poet who must consider all options must also consider how to sabotage them, even and perhaps especially when he is the poem's own "dictator," with the appropriately Latin meaning of "he whose word is law" intact. By making Ovid the ultimate mentor, Lowell has stealthily allowed himself

19. The Roman warrior Curtius volunteered to cast himself into a hitherto unfillable chasm in the forum; he fulfilled the prophecy that the chasm could not be closed except by throwing into it that upon which Rome's greatness was to be based. Lowell may be conflating this reference with one to Ernst Robert Curtius, a German cultural historian who touted Latin civilization as an answer to the chaos of Nazi Germany. Just as the cultural historian bases his theory of order on another, so Rome becomes literally "based" on the body of its fallen hero.

room to be changed into the human god of the poem, creator and reviser of his own identity, a poet who may not be immortal but who is at least still alive and "kicking" in his berth, while Santayana has not only died, but has also been immediately and surreptitiously replaced by a living poet who is flawed and human but "centred" in the individual self.

This particular version of "Beyond the Alps" goes the long way around to arrange for the final moving solitude of the poetic voice, a process that will be enacted again and again in the *Life Studies* manuscripts. In this version of "Beyond the Alps," Lowell pares ancient powers to human proportion, awards poets a powerful position in the state and proclaims them immortal, identifies himself with Santayana and then subtly disenfranchises the dead Santayana so that the living poet's voice is positioned to speak with newly won authority. Having worked out the process, Lowell can dismiss the apparatus in the version of "Beyond the Alps" that opens *Life Studies*. After establishing Santayana as mentor and guardian angel in earlier versions, Lowell sequesters him in another poem, "For George Santayana," and moves his persona without apology to the center of "Beyond the Alps."

A comparison of this famous poem with the previously examined versions shows how drastically various aspects of it have been reworked.[20] The poem's strategy is different from the start in that a papal decree, not Santayana's death, seems to inspire the reverie on the train from Rome to Paris. To feature a different event, the date has been moved back to "1950, the year Pius XII defined the dogma of Mary's bodily assumption," a revision which suggests that Lowell might have been thinking about the body of God's mother in connection with the death of his own. The new poem is much shorter than previous versions. The 1953 poem consists of seven fourteen-line stanzas, for example, while the *Life Studies* version is a scant three fourteen-line stanzas and a couplet. The later poem also differs in that

20. This poem is not a definitive "Beyond the Alps." Lowell used a version that includes the Ovid stanza in his next book, *For the Union Dead*, reminding us that for a poet in thrall to the shifting possibilities of language no poem is ever the final draft.

Lowell offers no explanation for the status of poets; he simply centers his persona as the perceiving eye. But now he is hardly a Juvenal tearing the Roman wolf mother to bits. She is not his mother after all, and as in the other versions of the poem, he is on the way out, escaping the bonds of her temporary custody. In this revision of "Beyond the Alps," Rome too has altered; it is a city of spectacle without the garish lighting, which seems to have moved into Santayana's poem with the "Blue" Catholic nuns. Here the "pure prose" Mussolini is once again "skirt-mad"; when he unfurls the eagle of Caesar, he seems, like Ovid of other versions, a human being about to bed down with power.

Most importantly, the section about Mary's assumption is energetically rewritten in the *Life Studies* version to match its importance in the poem's heading:

> The lights of science couldn't hold a candle
> to Mary risen—at one miraculous stroke,
> angel wing'd, gorgeous as a jungle bird![21]

While this is not to be believed ("But who believed this?") the adjectives fairly shimmer. Mary has not "risen to the realm of fact" but beyond, to a seductive exoticism. The words themselves are "gorgeous," and the transformation seems flooded with light; the rationality of science "couldn't hold a candle" to it. In this poem the evidence of power is not the beauty of the finished creation but the ability to wield a "miraculous stroke," to apotheosize through the persuasive power of language that which you name. This stroke Lowell claims for himself with the beauty of his language, and he claims it at last without benefit of tutor.

Yet Lowell as confident wielder of the miraculous strokes reminds us that for all its beauty such power is not to be trusted. He warns us against his own persuasiveness now that he is the undisputed subject of his poem, for all identity in language occurs within change, mutable and human. We too have undergone a metamorphosis as readers of the poem: we have become

21. Lowell, *Life Studies*, 4.

disciples marking proofs, and our hold on our identity is as jeopardized by the power of poetic language as if we were listening to the forceful voices of our parents, or any of our own early mentors. Santayana describes the authority of such language in the 1953 version of the poem when he boasts, "Essence took heart and landscape from my speech." Lowell's persona, "blear-eyed" and with his view circumscribed by the frame of a train window, has a more somber vision of the permutations that accrue around him and of his own control over them. As he watches, "Life changed to landscape." But either way the speaker is positioned at the heart of changing forms, which are the only possibility for articulating the self. The position is dangerous for both speaker and listeners, as the first is tempted to disperse himself in the rapid permutations represented by the shifting landscape outside the train window, while the others are tempted to give over their identities to the persuasive power of his voice.

Unlike Santayana, Lowell seems to grieve for what is lost in the transformations compelled by language and to mourn for the fixity of form he must disallow because it is finally an illusion. "There were no tickets for that altitude" where different versions of the powers he both yearns toward and flees ("prince, pope, philosopher, golden bough") are combined into one Goddess: Minerva, a type of divine mother from whom human beings are permanently orphaned. Yet Lowell knows that possession of this mother is impossible, and that it would not be good for us anyway. Her "pure mind" is as dangerous as "pure prose"; it is a "miscarriage of the brain" akin to madness.[22] Banned by his own knowledge from Minerva's heights, Lowell's persona has a compensatory vision. Through his window, which acts like Santayana's magnifying glass, the poet watches night change to day, nature's own miraculous transformation. He looked:

22. "Miscarriage of the brain" resonates suggestively with both Charlotte Lowell's fatal brain hemorrhage and Lowell's own bouts of mental illness. Both may also be related to the destructive "simplicity of mind" Lowell associated with "fanatical idealism."

> and saw Apollo plant his heels
> on terra firma through the morning's thigh . . .
> each backward, wasted Alp, a Parthenon,
> fire-branded socket of the Cyclops' eye.[23]

In the 1953 version of the poem, Lowell omits the third of these lines and begs Minerva to "decipher Europe" for him, to "vibrate through my pane," the last word of which is the boldest sort of homonym. In the *Life Studies* version of the poem, he has dismissed all such mentors and all such intercessory acts. Now even the most besieged of poets, even the most weary of observers, can transform a world imperfectly seen into a compelling succession of transcendently human stories.

The manuscripts of "Beyond the Alps" document Lowell's tortuous strategy for leaving behind that to which he is powerfully attracted—those persuasive mentors he must name and displace in order to establish his own shifting identity in his poems. Yet, the position gained, Lowell distrusts that power. Like the Pope's ability to send Mary winging to heaven, it is not quite to be believed. But in order to avoid the final fixity of silence, a poet is obliged to recreate himself in language despite, and through, his "pane." The mutability at the heart of all things is not only the poet's lone weapon, but also the ultimate source of his identity, a prize won from the divisions he himself creates. The power he thus unwillingly possesses pushes him into both unexpected dangers and unlooked for beauty. Even as Lowell abandons constricting forms and mourns the lack of safety everywhere, he peoples the landscape he flees in "Beyond the Alps" with powerful gods. If he himself is weary and imperfect of sight, his condition is as mutable as his vision, and another identity lies just ahead. In this version of "Beyond the Alps" it is represented by Paris, a city of light in which darkness shatters with the rising sun like a shape designed and then broken by a human hand.

When Lowell situated "Beyond the Alps" at the beginning of *Life Studies*, he provided an oblique clue to the strategies that shaped his volume. The drafts for "Beyond the Alps" show the

23. Lowell, *Life Studies*, 4.

poet revising away from what had shaped his earlier work—away from the high formalism of Allen Tate, from the anguished spirituality of George Santayana, from the lure of all those powerful mentors to whom he was always drawn, who were each, in his way, versions of Lowell himself. That he must resist the pull of these vivid presences in favor of a more mutable self, perpetually reborn in language of his own shaping, is the subtext of Lowell's revisions in this famous early *Life Studies* poem, and the process is reenacted again and again in the *Life Studies* drafts. He revises toward a vision of the self pulled toward both fixity and freedom, ultimately committed to the shifting middle ground that is the source of identity in language. In "Beyond the Alps" Lowell finally presents the scene of the dilemma as a moving landscape; the poet takes his place as that landscape's weary center, kicking at his "berth" as he looks both forward to Paris and back to Rome. When Lowell again takes up the problem, in the family material that becomes the core of *Life Studies,* he will call these ancient cities "Mother" and "Father."

2

CHANGING LIFE INTO LANDSCAPE

The Autobiographical Prose

Robert Lowell tells many bleakly humorous stories about dealing with Payne-Whitney's occupational therapy requirement during his 1954 stay, precipitated by the death of his mother earlier in the year. Set to various artistic tasks, Lowell found himself unable to translate thought into concrete form, a failure highly symbolic to someone whose life's work is writing. In one account, the embarrassment of not being able "to think with my hands" inspires Lowell to lie that he has the doctors' permission to read *Kim* instead. More often Lowell describes hopelessly botched products:

> Here for weeks I saw my abandoned pine-cone basket lying on the pile for waste materials. And as it sank under sawdust and shavings, it seemed to protest the pains Mr. Kemper, our instructor, had once taken to warp, to soak, to re-weave, to rescue it. And here in an old cigar box I saw my materially expensive, massively hideous silver ring, which Mr. Kemper had mostly forged and then capped off with an intaglio of an Iroquois corn shock ripening under the arrowy rays of a crescent moon.[1]

Such adventures in translating thought into form clearly pertain to Lowell's search for an appropriate new style, the search

1. Lowell, "At Payne Whitney," file 2227, Houghton Library. A version of these stories can be found in *Collected Prose*, 357–59.

that informed Lowell's work in the 1950s and found its culmination in *Life Studies*. As Lowell tells the Payne-Whitney story, he finally gravitates ("of course") to "young Miss Rodgers' painting class," and after a series of experiments in the styles of various artists, tries an imitation of Klee: "I used a formula that my Grandmother Winslow, Gaga, had taught me as a child. By making O's of different sizes and adding rectangles and a few dots, I could draw a picture which began as a farmhouse, a yard, a path and a pond; and then presto! was a man's face."[2]

That Lowell should situate this breakthrough experience in the art room, where "Life Studies" are traditionally done, suggests once again that the way back into life is through representation. And the way of drawing Lowell claims to rediscover here is a perfect paradigm of what the poet was looking for in his search for a "new style"—a seemingly transparent rendering that both hides and embodies the model, an abruptly human face. That the rendering is a childhood trick, taught by a grandmother who is literally "Gaga," is also peculiarly appropriate: Lowell's breakdown included a preoccupation with his early childhood, and his way out of the breakdown and into new poetic possibility would be to take over the power of the past by transcribing it. As the weary persona of "Beyond the Alps" would say, he had to learn how to change "Life" into "landscape" in order to recapture his own mysterious presence in both. In the process he would create a childhood version of the self that would both elucidate and challenge his beleaguered adult identity.

To describe childish things, Lowell would need childish tools; to the adult poet unable to write in his "old style," prose, the syntactic version of farmhouse, yard, path, and pond, seemed more appropriate for the task than did poetry. Lowell's discussions of prose characteristics are often confusing, but he clearly ascribed a certain simplicity to prose. It was a way of "rendering appearances," and he later said that the poems he reworked from prose for *Life Studies* were to seem "as open and single-surfaced as a photograph." This enterprise he linked to

2. Ibid.

rather surprising prose models: "That seems the perfect way, what War and Peace is . . .," and "I had in mind something like the prose of a Chekhov story."[3] From the vantage point of twenty years later, he would find this very quality of rendering appearances a "limitation," one "flattening to poetry's briefer genius." But at the time the method was almost palpably a relief. Home convalescing, Lowell describes the efficacious effect of writing prose as occupational therapy, a phrase that by this time can also be read as "help for my occupation":

> I sat looking out of my bedroom window at the Clinic and once more began to type at a poem, my substitute for the regulation Occupational Therapy requirement. I wrote:
>
> I was already half-way through my life
> When I woke up from Mother on the back
> Of the *Hill* in Boston, to a sky-line of Life
>
> Insurance buildings, still in blue-print.
>
> Then the labor, cynicism and maturity of writing in meter became horrible. I began to write rapidly in prose and in the style of a child.
>
> . . . name, Bobby Lowell. I was all of three and a half. My new formal gray shorts had been worn for all of three minutes.[4]

This account is as fascinating as it is disingenuous. Written after the fact, it offers a self-conscious diagram of Lowell's shift from the "labor" of poetry to the "rapidity" of prose, an effect flagged by the sudden appearance of "Bobby." That Lowell carefully demonstrates the varying dictions and chooses adult phrasing in order to reach his childhood self indicates he is well aware that "Bobby Lowell" is at least partly a fictional persona, one adopted for a particular technical effect. And because "Bobby" is so strategically circumscribed by his context and the

3. "A Conversation with Robert Lowell," interview with Ian Hamilton, 10; "Robert Lowell in Conversation with A. Alvarez," interview with A. Alvarez, 36.
4. Lowell, "Miscellaneous worksheets," file 2230, Houghton Library.

whole episode is told in the past tense, Lowell adroitly distances himself both from his childish persona and from the poet nearly desperate to reorganize his experience in language. The adult who narrates the present text is at pains to demonstrate that he is both cured of his childish delusions and in full control of his technique.

Yet even as a highly orchestrated retelling the passage offers intriguing evidence of what Lowell thought he was up to when, the long dry period ended, his mother dead and the poet himself reassembling his technique and his identity piece by piece, Lowell opened the floodgates to his past. The passage's poetry insert is an example of the constricting and laborious iambic pentameter that Lowell seeks to leave behind in his search for an appropriate new style. But the poetry is very instructive about what else Lowell must exclude from his therapeutic new venture. To remake his past and track his way back in the language of a new medium, Lowell must also evade more complex but equally pervasive habits.

The poetry insert identifies them cannily. One of the old habits is Lowell's almost compulsive allusiveness. The poem Lowell leaves stranded in the middle of his prose, for example, all too easily calls up Dante. Such allusions invite the associative depth Lowell was trying to avoid by his childlike stance and technique of "rendering appearances." Besides, the implied comparison between Lowell and Dante dragoons yet another authority figure into bolstering his position, a strategy Lowell is anxious to avoid, as he is in "Beyond the Alps," probably because it takes so many tortuous maneuvers to regain control of the poem. Here for safety's sake the rendering must seem transparent, an instantaneous recognition of being in the text via a "simple" arrangement that "presto! becomes a man's face."[5] The poetry insert outlines another danger as well. "When I woke up from Mother on the back" is almost thrillingly ambiguous, made more so by the rigid adherence to meter,

5. The word demonstrates both the orchestrated nature of the arrangement and the rapid transition between self and text: in music *presto* is an instruction to play rapidly, and the root word is the Latin *praestus*, "ready," from *praesto*, "at hand."

which spills "Of the *Hill* . . ." into the next line. The line suggests that the persona was in thrall to an almost hypnotizing mother and prefigures the presence of Charlotte Winslow Lowell as the most dangerously compelling presence in *Life Studies*. The power of the mother is in this case distinctly Oedipal, leading the poem not only into a quagmire of association, but into particularly unacceptable ones. The weight of such association, like that of allusions, immobilizes the forward narrative thrust of the poem as if it too were stunned into the volitionless state of its central ego. In the prose that quickly supersedes this careful retelling, Lowell picks a persona and a style that he believes will allow him to evade such depths: "all of three and a half," "Bobby Lowell" can follow a rapid narrative thread like a lifeline back to the time before he is cognizant of his own sexuality—back, in effect, to when it was still safe to sleep with Mother.

Because the abandoned bit of poetry is an early draft for the opening of "Sailing Home From Rapallo," the further implications are clear. Lowell also must wake from Mother because she is dead. He is left alone confronting "a sky-line of Life / Insurance buildings, still in blue-print," the break enforced by the meter once again demonstrating the painfully abrupt trapdoors into meaning that poetry is full of, and Lowell at this juncture finds it necessary to avoid. The switch into prose at this crucial point keeps Lowell from dealing with "the skyline of Life" as he escapes into a childish persona and "the style of a child." Literally, the poet is kept from writing the poem in which he will go back for his mother's body; by changing into "Bobby Lowell" he avoids not only the Oedipal suggestiveness of waking up from Mother but also the crucial fact that Mother herself is now asleep forever.

Lowell did eventually write about his mother's death, but the first accounts are in prose, suggesting, as does this segment of autobiographical prose with the embedded poem, that to talk about his mother's death Lowell had to go the long way around. In the final structure of *Life Studies*, this reading is reinforced by the carefully ordered sequence of the volume's "Life Studies" section. The prose that Lowell began "in the style of a child" after he abandoned the early draft of "Sailing Home From

Rapallo" became the first poem of the "Life Studies" section and one of Lowell's most famous poems in the "new style": "My Last Afternoon With Uncle Devereux Winslow." Lowell thus used the prose to work his way in from the dead at the periphery of the family. After the poem about his mother's dead brother, Lowell positioned poems about his mother's dead parents and his mother's dead husband, before the poem in which the persona, unobtrusively grown up, must come to terms with the crucial dead body of the mother. Then the torch passes from generation to generation before our eyes in "During Fever," in which mother and son seem to be reborn as father and daughter, and the persona takes us through a variety of domestic interiors before he emerges in "Skunk Hour" to confront a mother and her children who are decidedly "other."

For all the circuitousness of this strategy, Lowell seems to think of the autobiographical prose as a way back to psychological and occupational health. The fact that Lowell includes a section of his autobiographical prose in his developing manuscript as "91 Revere Street" attests to his continuing belief in the power of prose, as does a lone story composed in the sixties that revisits the childhood material in more fictional form.[6] Yet despite the reputed appropriateness of his prose, Lowell goes back through his autobiographical material and transforms whole sections into a block of startling new poems. One possible explanation for the reworking of prose into poetry is that Lowell needs to demonstrate within the structure of *Life Studies* itself that he is past the necessity of writing in prose (a point, ironically, he is able to make only by writing the prose first). He has worked his way back through the new medium and through childhood to poetry and to the skyline of adult life. In this reading the structure of *Life Studies* is strategic indeed. Having demonstrated what he wishes to leave behind stylistically in the first section of *Life Studies* (all reworked early poems), Lowell shakes himself free of his old style and into his early memories in the prose of "91 Revere Street"; he dedicates the third section

6. I consider the "The Raspberry Sherbet Heart" in the June 1993 issue of *Shenandoah* (vol. 43, no. 2).

to friends and mentors as if to demonstrate that he is living, healthy, and working; and finally, fully in charge of his material, he moves purposefully, if somewhat beleagueredly, to the center of his work as its protagonist, a process surely as laborious as that by which Lowell's "blear-eyed ego" takes over the central position in "Beyond the Alps."[7]

But this reading, while it has the narrative logic the fifties prose convert Lowell might well enjoin us to accept, overlooks the ambivalence at the heart of Lowell's efforts in prose. Lowell would like us to believe that his prose was written "in the style of a child" and therefore circumvents the "labor, cynicism and maturity" of writing not only in meter, but with the particularly painful suggestiveness that is poetry's stock-in-trade. He would like us to believe, correspondingly, that his persona has achieved a magical breakthrough back into childhood with the sudden appearance of "Bobby" in the text. But of course Lowell writes as an adult, and both child and adult versions of the self occupy the same space on the page in the familiar manner of all retrospective life stories. The prose is therefore prone to the same unwilling realizations about the nature of the self that complicate the poetry. By attempting to write as a child, Lowell is actually caught once again in the dilemma of competing presences—and once that happens, he has given up any hopes of writing without associative depth, of writing in a way that can confine itself to "rendering appearances." He has imported into his prose the same dualities that fuel his poetry.

This inherent multiplicity of perspective is easily demonstrated by Lowell's characters, especially the doubled self he presents in his autobiographical prose. And once again Lowell demonstrates his dilemma not only in his characters but in his technical choices. It is particularly revealing, for example, that he makes conflicting claims for prose: prose can both move freely and rapidly as it skims lightly across the surface of experience, or it can be single-surfaced as a photograph, a

7. Both Stephen Yenser and Ian Hamilton have made versions of the argument that Lowell narrows the focus of *Life Studies* to a study of the individual at the end of the book; see Yenser, *Circle to Circle*, 122–55, and Hamilton, *Robert Lowell*, 263.

description that implies fixity. These arguments recall Lowell's attraction both to the highly metrical and the highly free in his poetry, assuring that his prose will be as torn between possibilities as his more usual medium.

The tension is enacted at every level in Lowell's autobiographical prose. Most overtly, many of the reminiscences are about places that are transitional and not quite home: the unhappy sojourn in Washington when Charlotte Lowell longed to be in Boston, Lowell's time away at school, the family's summer stays at his Grandfather Winslow's summer house, and Lowell's own adult retreats to the asylum.[8] While only the accounts of "Rock," the family name for the citadel of the grandfather, seem relatively happy, to be metaphorically and literally between places as these times seem to have been is an opportunity for a painful rebirth of the self akin to that offered by the hurtling train in "Beyond the Alps." At least it is a state associated with life rather than death, we remind ourselves as the body count climbs in *Life Studies*. Stylistically, Lowell tries to deal with these stories of times between in what he thinks of as the narrative rapidity and syntactic clarity of prose. However, his task is subverted because he structures the material around the unmovable figure of Charlotte Lowell.

Secure in the Boston of Lowell's youth, fixed forever by being dead, the poet's mother is the unchanging star around whom the satellites group, set into motion by her changeless vigor. The prose account of the Lowells' attempt to find a school for the problematic Bobby is typical of the dynamic: "I was promised an improved future and taken on Sunday afternoon drives through the suburbs to inspect the boys' schools: Rivers, Dexter, Country Day. These expeditions were stratagems designed to give me a chance to know my father; Mother noisily stayed behind and amazed me by pretending that I had forbidden her to embark on 'men's work.'" Bob Lowell, Senior, does all the driving, but it is clear that from her Boston stronghold Charlotte is the family mover and shaker. She criticizes the results of these

8. See the following files in the Houghton Library collection: "Washington D.C. 1924," file 2221; "Entering St. Mark's," file 2224; "Rock," file 2220; "The balanced aquarium," file 2226; and "At Payne Whitney," file 2227.

enforced male outings and goes back to interview the headmasters herself: "she expressed astonishment that a wishy-washy desire to be everything to everybody had robbed a naval man of any reliable concern for his son's welfare."[9]

When the family does move because of the needs not of the mother but of the father, the results are fatal. Lowell's parents move to a new house at "Beverly Farms" after one of Bob Lowell's heart attacks, and at first the change seems beneficial. The father is now "vitally trim" and reminds Lowell of Eisenhower, something of an authority figure at last. At this juncture Bob Lowell dies of his final heart attack: the move has been a poignantly deceptive illusion of flexibility and freedom. Bob Lowell's control over the family's movements is as vestigial as one of his unfashionable automobiles; the shift to Beverly Farms is finally as fruitless as the series of mishaps by which his son arrives in Rapallo too late to see his mother alive.

Despite a flight across the surface of experience attempted in what Lowell considered a liberating medium, the story told by the autobiographical prose is that power lies at the fixed center. Robert Lowell's many descriptions of his mother invoke her stability as the family's reigning presence. This one is a fragment from the "Miscellaneous worksheets" section of his unpublished prose:

> I might have been fifteen or I might have been thirty-five, my father might have been alive or he might have been dead, the location might have been our good (not grand) half a life-time's house in the Back Bay, or Mother's adequate Boston apartment, or Mother and Father's sprawly, slightly citified, unbalanced, battle-ship gray commuters' house in Beverly Farms, where they had migrated towards the end for a change, and of course changed as little as possible. Thus, one didn't start with a place or even a room that could be labelled such and such and no other. You had to begin with Mother's furniture, and *that* didn't change at all—if it did, the new or different pieces always managed to retell the same story.[10]

9. Lowell, *Life Studies*, 27–28.

10. Lowell, "Miscellaneous worksheets," file 2230, Houghton Library. In the manuscript, "he might have been" in the first sentence has a line drawn through it.

The effect of this controlling presence on the child and then man who is her son drives Lowell to make the type of allusive parallels he knows are dangerous. On the same page of the manuscript, Lowell acts out a nearly physical battle to stay on the surface of his story and momentarily fails. The lapse comes after an almost hysterical summoning of the voices of male authority figures (Valéry and Freud), who advise the susceptible not to put much store in the old myths. Lowell is immediately plunged into a struggle not to identify his mother and himself as Clytemnestra and Orestes:

> Now to get back to my subject. I am writing about one person and not two,[11] and it would be stupidly overstepping myself to call this person Clytemnestra and empty out a whole picture book of far-fetched parallels, such as the only child who held the center of the stage till the age of five, the jut-chinned sister of the plastic Helen, the grave ignorant bride of the unknown great king and so on and so on down to, God help us, matricide. I am now waving my arms so wildly that I forget what I am proposing not to propose. Shall I say that all the phases of Clytemnestra, crown of the moon, from tender young slip to haft of the battle axe were chips off the same old block? The old wooden mask?

Lowell gets himself out of danger in this disturbing account of the mother's power by reciting the curious story of a man who at age five knew all of Beethoven and Stravinsky and then trains himself to forget what he used to know by a type of self-hypnosis. He looks at so many Greek statues that he ends up asking "Who was the Greeks?" For the sake of his identity as it is embodied in his writing, Lowell must stay away from "the Greeks" and all such dangerous allusions, or trick himself into a type of forgetfulness. Despite his claims for the salubriousness of prose, this passage demonstrates that the new medium can

11. With this remark Lowell seems to be willing himself away from multiplicity and toward what he thinks of as a proselike simplicity in considering his powerful parent. Later in this sentence, on the other hand, "picture book" has been crossed out in the manuscript and "art cataloge" printed overhead, as if to will the diction back into an appropriately adult form.

lead him all too easily into the same treacherous ground as did poetry.

The aforementioned passages also make it clear that the power of the more fixed position, which is associated with all unyielding figures from "fanatical idealists" down to his own mother, always threaten to engulf the more mutable, and hence less stable, versions of the self. When Lowell writes about Payne-Whitney, he sometimes describes himself and the other inmates as fish in a "balanced aquarium," a fluid world held captive within a more structured one. The metaphorical resemblance to the conditions of a created but unborn child are clear, and in a more threatening formulation, the architecture that surrounds the poet is itself threateningly female: "First I saw the hospital's architecture as wedding-cake; no, not a wedding cake but the tall bride standing with her sacrificial silver knife beside the wedding cake; no, not the bride of flesh and blood, but a narrow, late Gothic bride, all arches, groins and stone lacework; no bride, but a building. . . ."[12]

Lowell writes himself away from dangerous associations by an effort of will in this passage, too, but it is well worth identifying the bride who seems to engulf him on all sides. In another version of this episode, the bridal building is linked to the bridal photograph his father keeps on his dresser, and in the drafts of "Sailing Home from Rapallo," the dead mother is also a bride. The powerful mother holds the son at the center, but for him the position is fraught with peril: he is trapped almost as if he had been ingested by the bridal buildings of the New York Hospital, which remind him of the all-powerful center of his world.

It would thus appear that for Lowell the position of most power is one that is psychologically untenable because it would force a fatal identification with his mother. One possible coping mechanism might be an appropriation of her position, a strategy that Lowell enacts symbolically in those stories reported by Hamilton from the autobiographical prose when young Bobby Lowell swallows a jewelry elephant or drops a lost crucifix into

12. Lowell, "The balanced aquarium," file 2226, Houghton Library. *Collected Prose* offers a version of this description (346).

the furnace, the center of his parents' house.[13] When the boy ingests these objects he tries to control literally what is at his body's center. At the same time he acts out symbolically what it means to be a woman, holding a precious object in his midmost region as his mother once held him, living but captive.

Certainly the project is doomed from the start, for the real object of his desire is impossible to attain. Freudian and Lacanian readings of such an attempt remind us that such objects are compensation for the original moment of division and loss in which the ego is born: "A primordially split subject necessitates an originally lost object." The situation is always made clear when a male ego considers female sexuality, for the original division between sexes "confirms that the subject is split and the object is lost."[14] Mother is the original model of female sexuality in a child's world; she recalls the original split most powerfully, and therefore any object her son tries to keep from her, including his own identity, is impossible to hang on to for very long. Surely the results of Bobby Lowell's endeavors are rather ignominious, especially in the case of the elephant, which reappears after a few days in the obvious manner. Such attempts at control are the doomed stratagems of a defiant child, and the man who reports them seems to laugh at his naiveté, or at least he reports that Charlotte Lowell certainly did: "I have no idea how Mother managed to mention the chamberpot, my movement, and the marvelous elephant all in one pure, smirking breath."[15]

No matter how bold or devious the young boy's attempted takeover of her position, the only person who can control the center is Mother, a moral that is acted out by an incident Hamilton omits:

> This is my first remembered meeting with my grandfather, and I know that it was my birthday because I see him standing beside a present from my father, a flotilla of little camouflaged wooden

13. Hamilton, *Robert Lowell*, 228–30. The elephant story is also reported in *Collected Prose*, 307–8.
14. Lacan, *Feminine Sexuality*, 25.
15. Lowell, "Ante-bellum Boston," file 2209, Houghton Library.

> warships that had been laid out along the mantle piece. They had been purchased in the name of, and as a tribute to, my father who was off on sea-duty. Like later presents from my father, these toys had been bought with considerable pains and were a remarkable bargain, and very unfeminine. Made in Japan the boats were outrageously anti-German: the best boat was an American hostal ship magnificently marked with warning red crosses. By pressing a button on a cord, a concealed spring mouse-trapped shut and the cabins and turrets of the hospital ship collapsed on the floor—it had been hit by sub-marine's torpedo. . . . However, the toy was meant for adults and my mother soon robbed it of all allure. She snatched it from my hands, disembowelled it of its dangerous spring, and then gave its back, weightless and harmless, an insipid husk of its former warlike outrages.[16]

Mother's action is clearly castrating, and the father who is "off on sea duty" is so far away from the powerful center that he is unable to prevent the disemboweling (literally "taking away the guts"; the pun on the "gutless" father would not be lost on Lowell) of his "unfeminine" present. In this version of the story, the father's ownership of the ships in the first place is obliquely called into question. "They were purchased in the name of, and as a tribute to, my father" implies that either the mother bought them herself in the father's name and then sabotaged them before her son's eyes, or that the masculine present had something to do with the grandfather's arrival. The latter reading suggests other versions of the incident, in which the maternal grandfather is upheld as the representative of Bobby's, and hence of masculine, interest: ". . . I still enjoy in recollection the feeling of relief I experienced when he scolded and teased my mother for ruining a flotilla of toy warships."[17] In this version the set is not only a bargain, but "imperceptibly damaged," already flawed before the mother "ruins" it. And here the flagship is described not only as a "hostal ship" but more

16. Lowell, "Ante-bellum Boston," file 2209, Houghton Library. In the manuscript, "remembered meeting" in the first sentence of this excerpt has "image" printed above it. The ellipis points in this quotation indicate my omission rather than Lowell's own punctuation.

17. Lowell, "Ante-bellum Boston," file 2209, Houghton Library. *Collected Prose* also includes a version of this story (305–6).

specifically as a "hospital ship." When the spring works, "the hospital ship with all its gear, cabins, cots, stretchers and even red-cross nurses collapsed on the carpet." The mother thwarts this gory function when she gouges out the spring, taking away the ship's center—which may be a "mousetrap" but also acts as a peculiar escape mechanism for the inhabitants of the floating hospital.

Her action suggests not only that Mother controls the center of power, but that she administers all escape routes as well. Of course, the reference to "hospital" (in still other manuscripts the boat is a German U-boat) suggests Lowell's own various incarcerations. By removing the boat's spring for her own purposes, the mother has absconded with both the powerful center and the only possibility for release from it. That the ship is a "hospital" suggests that what is at stake may be mental health. Grown all powerful, the mother who wields such authority must be actively resisted. Her presence is suggestively pervasive: in a fragment from the autobiographical prose filed under "Rock," she appears in the sitting room in pink nightclothes, and the son feels her inappropriate sexual pull. "Pink was to be held in Mother's bedroom. But here she was spilling out like a jack-in-the-box with too powerful a spring." If the secret box suggests femininity, the spring is the male weapon from the gunboat; the motif has been reworked to show that when Mother possesses such a powerful device she is far more dangerous than any toy. In her presence, Lowell says, "I felt meshed and menaced."[18]

Mother's control over her son both as child and as adult seems complete in the powerfully symbolic stories of the ruined gift from the father. But in the Christmas stories, the opposing presence of the grandfather demonstrates not only Lowell's obvious admiration and affection for the family's most powerful male, but also what a male who seems to have escaped the castrating effects of Mother's sexuality would look like. Arthur Winslow fearlessly chides the mother on the child's behalf; even more important, he carries a potent talisman of the

18. Lowell, "Rock," file 2220, Houghton Library.

type young Bobby continually covets but only temporarily possesses.

> Arthur Winslow, my mother's father, paid us a surprise visit in 1919 a day or so before Christmas. I was almost three years old and I remember him distinctly. He was certainly wearing a white starched colar and a gray white tie-pin. Not only that, but he had a mysterious gold match-box dangling like the grapes of Tantalus from his gold watch chain. And I know that I wanted to own that match-box, and wasn't to be distracted by my legitimate Christmas present, a little flotilla a camouflaged wooden warships.[19]

Bobby Lowell is barred from the possession of this "mysterious" masculine talisman, which like the jack-in-the-box, combines adorned exterior with hidden power. He both yearns for it and feels responsible for it, as in this passage in which Lowell identifies the matchbox with that other metaphorically similar object sabotaged when his father was "off on sea duty":

> Meanwhile my grandfather walked up and down in front of the fireplace and snapped his gold match-box open and shut. Somehow I imagined that the U-boat's spring was now inside the match-box, which had the added glories of being true gold, able to burst into flame, and none of the pettiness and unreality of objects solely designed as toys for children. I have a nightmare memory of the matchbox disappearing. All morning I seem to have folding and unfolding a heavy sheet of brown wrapping paper. I kept holding the paper up to the fireplace and hoping to see the matchbox outlined against its brown tranlucentcy. I had a panicky feeling that my attitude and method of searching was wrong, that the matchbox lay hidden somewhere in the paper, and that only my headlong, cllous temper prevented it from being promtly revealed. The matchbox never re-appeared, and soon even its mechanics later seemed fabulous, improbable and impossible—a matchbox of gold that flew open by pressing a button and which lit like a cigarette lighter. How often I used for the next six or seven years to introduce it unbelievable into

19. Lowell, "Ante-bellum Boston," file 2209, Houghton Library. "To spoil my contentment with Christmas" is handwritten above the last sentence of this passage.

> questions addressed to my grandfather, whenever he was in a gay mood, nor would I ever be appeased by being allowed to handle his watch chain with the snake head hook, or even his watch itself.[20]

In these incidents both the mother and her father have acquired symbols of power within, whether by natural right of possession or, in the case of the mother, by a co-opting act. Lowell feels the lack of these objects acutely, and the suspicion is that the loss of them is somehow his fault. The boy who must resort to devious questioning or downright stealth to obtain them clearly does not feel he has the right to their potent magic.[21] But in his grandfather he can see their power at work, even though he knows himself to be shut out from it. Consequently, Lowell yearns toward and longs to identify with his maternal grandfather as he must not identify with his mother: "Grandpa! Have me, hold me, cherish me!" he cries in "Grandparents." But the grandfather is already implicated with the mother (he is her "Freudian papa," Lowell claims in "During Fever"), and he is in any case far beyond the child's powers of imitation: Bobby is made more feminine rather than more masculine in the presence of this role model. In "Dunbarton," the child persona "cuddled like a paramour" in his grandfather's bed, more like an illegal lover than the legitimate progeny of the powerful grandfather, whose fire-building skills in "Dunbarton" recall the manuscripts' hidden "matchbox."[22]

Lowell also takes his search for tokens of power he cannot possess outside the family circle in the autobiographical prose, indicating that his yearning for an originally lost object is a condition of his presence in the world at large. In "My Crime Wave" Lowell tells of various childhood "thefts": of stealing marbles, of tricking an acquaintance into trading valuable toy soldiers for worthless papier-mâché ones, of shoplifting a toy microscope. In each case the theft goes somehow awry, as if the child subconsciously knows such objects are not to be his. He is

20. Ibid.

21. Such objects often appear in fairy tales to rescue their protagonists, indicating that we understood their power long before Freud.

22. Lowell, *Life Studies*, 69, 80, 67.

found out, or in the case of the toy microscope, the elaborately acquired object doesn't work (this last contingency embroils Lowell in a complicated plot to return the flawed microscope to the store for a refund). The fun Lowell pokes at his child persona is rather merciless in these manuscripts, as merciless as Mother's mention of young Bobby's treasure-filled bowel movement. The self-mocking tone leads to some painful effects, none more so than when Lowell claims that the thefts were less for the sake of the objects than to achieve solidarity with a confederate: "'Every day, in every way, I am becoming a better and better friend to Werner Ash,' this is how I ended my prayers each night." It is almost as if the companion is here the desired object, but the friendships gained by such "furtive, spectacular safe, risks" are as fleeting as the thrill of acquiring the objects themselves. Lowell tells of cooperating with Werner Ash in a ruse to win eight hundred marbles and then tricking Werner in turn: "The way I did this was . . . well, to tell the truth, Werner was a little less everything than I was: less strong, less unpopular, less stubborn, less a c-minus student, less a child of fortune less his mother's son."[23]

The friendship that depends on inherent inequality is doomed, the statement implies, much as Lowell's touting of powerful mentors is always a device that insures their loss of power. Once tricked, Werner Ash is not a longed-for friend but weaker prey, a quality the "mother's son" must be true to himself by taking advantage of, just as the strong must always dominate the weak. The fragile object that is the boyhood friendship cannot withstand such scrutiny. The unsatisfactory thefts and friendships of "My Crime Wave," like the hidden matchbox and the disgorged spring of the family stories, suggest again that while Lowell anxiously covets such talismans, he knows they are not for him. Recovered by rightful owners or rendered inoperable in Lowell's possession, such objects, the suggestion is, must be kept from him: the center of power they represent must be

23. Lowell, "My Crime Wave," file 2223, Houghton Library. The words "less his mother's son" have been added by hand. Note how Lowell reconstructs his friend's advantages over him as disadvantages.

hidden safely elsewhere to prevent attempted co-option by the endlessly desiring self.

The burden of these stories is perpetual loss, but Lacan would remind us that language is born in just this way: words are what we create to stand in for our lost objects.[24] For a writer the loss is particularly emblematic because words are also the signs of his power. Loss thus has its material compensation in Lowell's stories about it, and interestingly enough the poet who tells his story in the autobiographical prose does obtain a talisman reminiscent of his childhood yearning when he is permitted fingernail clippers: "For the first time in the two months since my acceptance by the Clinic, I enjoyed 'sharps-priviledges.'"[25] The nail clippers Lowell recovers are hardly the exotic tokens of childhood, the magical matchbox, or the toy boat with its dangerous spring. They are a homely reward for returning health—a weapon, the prohibition against them suggests, that he is no longer in danger of using against himself. But Lowell seems to have learned a lesson about the central power represented by such objects. As a child Lowell was nearly sick with desire to own what he could not keep. As an adult he knows the advantages of freeing things of the constrictions imposed by his identity. "I pulled the dingy, disfiguring adhesive tape marked 'Lowell' from my nail clipper, and saw the whole morning flash blindingly from the chromium surface." Here to strip his identity from the tokens of power is to be gifted with an Emersonian vision of the blinding wholeness of something outside the self, a vision that momentarily compensates for all loss.

The many talismans of Lowell's autobiographical prose suggest a potent moral about the divided self. The symbol of the power at the center that he must not possess is imaged in Freudian terms as the mother, and to be free of her is to experience the partial loss of his own identity. To develop an identity that could stand on equal terms with the mother yet remain beyond her castrating power is to be masculine—to be, in short,

24. Lacan, *Feminine Sexuality*, 31.
25. Lowell, "Miscellaneous worksheets," file 2230, Houghton Library.

a father. We have seen that Lowell's maternal grandfather is Lowell's candidate for the role. It is he who defends the absent father's Christmas present and who displays aggressively masculine symbols: tie-pin, matchbox, and, in other manuscripts, a phallic walking stick that the young Lowell "borrows." In the manuscripts of the poem "Dunbarton," Lowell even writes out the presence of the disapproving father and shifts the poem's substance wholly over to the grandfather, who "Loved to release his clutch / And coast on the worst Dunbarton roads," a dangerously masculine freedom from restraint that "My father could never understand."[26]

In the finished poem this father is absent once again, adroitly replaced in all but name by the "proper" parent:

> When Uncle Devereux died
> Daddy was still on sea-duty in the Pacific;
> it seemed spontaneous and proper
> for Mr. MacDonald, the farmer,
> Karl, the chauffeur, and even my Grandmother
> to say, "your Father." They meant my Grandfather.
>
> He was my Father. I was his son.[27]

But this identification involves psychological risk for the boy who huddles, at the end of the poem, in the bed of his mother's "Freudian papa," not as if he were the grandfather's son, but the mother herself. To withstand the fatal temptation to identify with his mother, Lowell needs a father who is not also his mother's father, and to this end he tries on, in *Life Studies*, the often unprepossessing figure of Bob Lowell as the source of his identity.

Lacan's explanation of the way language works depends on his argument that symbolic order is derived from the replacement of the mother by the paternal signifier, the "Name-of-the Father."[28] Robert Lowell, a son named after his father, did claim that the *Life Studies* poems were grouped around that parent, an

26. Lowell, "Dunbarton," file 2193, Houghton Library.
27. Lowell, *Life Studies*, 65.
28. Silverman, *The Subject of Semiotics*, 131, 190.

assessment that at first seems skewed in a consideration of the manuscripts, in which the mother's character is so pervasive. "Unanswerable Motherhood!" Lowell exclaims at one point, as if throwing up his hands at her character's perfect power. But while *Life Studies* often seems to orbit around the fixed center represented by the all-too-present mother, the never-quite-there father acts as a contrapuntal force and a strategy for identification of the self outside the mother.[29] Lowell's prose manuscripts twice break into poems about the father, much like the already quoted section that attempts a poem about the mother before it weans itself back to prose health. These efforts demonstrate the psychological and technical difficulties incurred by making the elusive father a model for his son's identity, and they document Lowell's eventual identification with that problematic figure.

In one version of the poetry/prose experiment that tries to organize itself around the father as a center of power, Lowell is interrupted at his desk by "Prince Scharnhorst," a hospital inmate. Lowell hides a piece of paper on which he'd written the first and last lines of a sonnet entitled:

TO MY FATHER

You sailed to China, Father, and knew your math . . .
Friendly to all, and loving none, perhaps.[30]

The prose then switches into a detailed description of the prince and the father disappears from the text except for the presence in his place of a toy boat, which the prince offers to lend Lowell because Lowell's father, "a naval man, had admired Count von Luckner, the Sea Devil." This miniature is another token provided in place of the absent father. Like the other tokens, this one cannot be Lowell's own: it is to borrow, not to keep. The

29. Lowell, "- - -," file 2225, Houghton Library. Jay Martin has argued for both patterns in "Grief and Nothingness: Loss and Mourning in Lowell's Poetry," 36. I think that Mother and Father must battle it out even in the book's larger structure, and that Lowell's grief is at least partly a result of this aspect of his creation of their characters.

30. Lowell, "At Payne Whitney," file 2227, Houghton Library.

father himself has disappeared; the prince takes over the text as the story's controlling presence, one that is as vibrant as Mother in her pink nightgown: "He flamed in my doorway, a sunbeam—a man so various in his moonshines and virtuousity that I half imagined he was an apparition, an actor." In this version of the prose that offers an embedded poem, the figure of Lowell's father has been appropriated by that of the colorful Prince Scharnhorst, who now seems to control both the story and the talisman that recalls the father. If this appropriation acts as a sudden end to the power of the father in the story, it is one prefigured by the poetry insert. This "hidden" manuscript acts as its own cogent dismissal: the sonnet form has been reduced to a summary couplet, the first descriptive line of which is itself overpowered by the dismissive bite of the conclusion.

The unexpected force of this dismissal depends on the central paradox of the father's character. Unlike the figure of the mother, whose "furniture" never changes, the figure of Lowell's father, "Friendly to all, and loving none, perhaps," is essentially mysterious. Appearances aren't useful, in his case, as keys to the inner man; the smile Lowell describes elsewhere as "anxious" and "repetitive" does not necessarily indicate love. If the father loves "none," then he is without tie to them; he is free from their power, psychologically absent wherever he goes. But it is a terrible thing for a child, even a grownup one, to acknowledge that his parent might not love him, and the man who writes the bitterly concise couplet provides only the most minimal of escape routes from the awful possibility in the last "perhaps." Robert Lowell, Senior, despite his seeming powerlessness in those sections of the autobiographical prose in which his ineffectiveness is contrasted with the power of the mother, emerges in this couplet as a figure who wields a mysterious authority of his own. While the mother is consuming, and all identification with her is psychologically dangerous, the father is no help either against the mother or as a role model because he is an enigma, as inaccessible to Lowell as those mysterious talismans of his youth. The resulting dilemma is particularly painful, though some version of it is familiar to every grownup child who has undergone the necessary separation of his or her identity from that of the parents.

In Lowell's *Life Studies* manuscripts, the necessary division from the opposite poles of identity represented by his parents has become the spring that powers the autobiographical material. At the period of Lowell's life in which he writes of his parents, they are already dead, but as he goes back to the past and restructures his identity through his language he has already situated his persona psychologically as an orphan: one whose identity must be kept apart from the mother's, but whose rightful role model has effectually removed himself from the scene.

The manuscript that begins with Lowell writing a hidden poem in the hospital therefore demonstrates the uselessness of the enigmatic father as a source of personal power. Another version of the task leads Lowell to the same conclusion, though by a radically different method. In this version of the prose/poetry experiment, Lowell situates himself as a remembering adult:

> My mind moved through the pictures of conscience, and remained in its recollections, weightless, floating; *in media res*! I remembered the red storm lights and the brown tobacco spaces of night and the city's sky. On a sallow sheet of onion-skin paper, whose semi-transparency half-revealed and half concealed the pink pads of my fingers and the royal blue abacadabra of the blotter; I wrote:
>
> In Boston the Hancock Life Insurance Building's
> beacon flared
> Foul weather, Father, as far as to the Charlestown
> Naval Yard
> And almost warmed. . . .[31]

One of the problems with this poem as a showcase of the father's power is that, like the manuscript poem about the mother that is surrounded by prose, this too is an early draft of "Sailing Home from Rapallo." Here Father is adrift in the story of Lowell's mother's death, a story that overwhelms him in importance. Even the metaphoric suggestion that the persona sees the landscape as a sailor would, in other words as his dead father would, does not keep the poem going: the last line trails

31. Ibid.

off as if aware that its sense is dispersing, and the prose switches into a description of the night "when Mother was dying all alone at that little private hospital in Rapallo." On that night "the needle of the Hancock Life Insurance Building was flashing storm warnings." The image from the poem has been rewritten as prose, and the following paragraph of reminiscence takes us through various settings of familial importance to the family graveyard, where the father is already buried, something of an intruder "unless he produced a dead wife, a Winslow."[32] What follows is a moving account of Lowell's time in Rapallo, and the prose Lowell summons for the purpose will eventually be reworked as "Sailing Home from Rapallo," the one published version of Lowell's confrontation with his mother's death. (I discuss the transformation of this poem more thoroughly in Chapter 3.)

In both instances the father is rendered useless to Lowell, and the switch into prose serves to prove the point. If prose helps Lowell control the associations surrounding the mother, the same strategy with regard to the father works all too similarly, and all too well. By one method or another the father is overpowered in the text and either vanishes into a new form or is kept "hidden." The boy who needs a response to the sway of "unanswerable Motherhood" is unable to find it in the mysterious person of the father, whose central enigma turns out to be as "unanswerable" as the mother's clear authority.

Lowell's attempt to put the figure of his father at the heart of *Life Studies* is showcased in "91 Revere Street," the prose centerpiece of the finished *Life Studies* volume. This prose passage has had many fine readings, and Vereen Bell's assertion that in "91 Revere Street" the prose technique is a disingenuous way of forcing the appearance of unity while simultaneously undermining any such possibility is central to my own reading. Lowell's ambivalence about the enigma that is his father is mirrored in his aforementioned ambivalence about prose itself: the idea that prose progress is both rapid and motionless, like the idea of the father who "smiles on all, loving none, perhaps,"

32. The words "a dead" have been inserted by hand in the typescript.

is relentlessly paradoxical. It is no surprise, then, that prose constructed around the father "forces transitions across the flimsiest of associations" and is filled with details which "radiate implication" but elude understanding.[33] It is no wonder, I would extend the argument, that prose constructed around problematic centers of power must always act very much like lyric poetry.

Earlier manuscripts help get to the source of Lowell's ambivalence about both the subject and the medium of his autobiographical material and lead back to the problematic father. "91 Revere Street" is a compilation of several manuscript sources, and Lowell combines and shapes them so they are loosely structured around the figure of Bob Lowell. However, the father has a particularly potent rival in the grandfather. The collection of manuscripts grouped under the heading "Rock," many of which begin with the ringing and mysterious "I don't want to go anywhere; I want to go to Rock" offers the beleaguered central figure's response to the fact that, as Charlotte Lowell is made to say, "Bobby adores his Grandfather."[34] Robert Lowell, Senior, "was almost bitterly bored by my obsession" with his wife's father, and Lowell gives him credit for an uncomfortable parental insight when "Mother was away, and he thought I was out of earshot": "Rock, Rock, Rock," he said, "my boy is a rock-bottom Puritan. I wonder when his Grandfather will learn that he dislikes anything anyone else likes?" The rivalry between father and grandfather in young Bobby's affections is ruefully clear here, as is the child's guilty preference. Both men, however, believe that the self can be reframed and improved: Grandfather provides endless activities that bespeak "better selves" abundantly and for all, while the father reads on his own "books on self-instruction" from which the child is excluded.[35] Lowell would like some instruction on the subject, but his father effectively puts him off. As Lowell claims with forceful pseudo-nonchalance: "Always, he seemed to treat me as though I were some relation of Mother's who was visiting.

33. Vereen Bell, *Robert Lowell: Nihilist as Hero*, 52–54, 51–52.
34. Lowell, "Rock," file 2220, Houghton Library.
35. "Finest" is printed above "better."

He could remember my Christian name and even my nicknames, but somehow or other my surname had escaped. He would rather have had his fingernails pulled one by one than have said anything to me that was impolite, called for, or fatherly."[36]

As an adult, Lowell will remember pulling his name off his nail clippers as a gesture of freedom, but the father's efforts to free him from the Lowell name and male bloodline and to make him a "relation of Mother's" is confusing and painful to Bobby. Lowell prefers his rocklike grandfather, and the implied rivalry between the two male grownups for the boy's affection, with the mother clearly on her father's side, is not an attractive story—a fact Lowell seems to recognize later in the account, when his mother perceives that Bobby's own "better self wished we would drop dead."[37] He later crossed out the following:

> I feel a need t splash some whitewash on this picture. Things weren't, of course, all this bad. I have always liked that unimaginable Hieronymous Bosch expression about "the pot painting the kettle black." No less monstrous and grotesque is the picture of a writer in extremis, the writer inspired to give himself black eyes because there is no one else in range, no other way to fill the page . . .

After this excised confession in which he shifts the blame for domestic disharmony onto his own shoulders by making it a writer's problem, Lowell begins a version of "91 Revere Street" with the comment "Yet there once really was a day, when I just about wished every one would drop dead." What follows is a version of the dinner party that closes "91 Revere Street," one in which the confrontations are more overt than they are in the polished *Life Studies* account, and in which the child actively, guiltily, participates. As Lowell says often, he considered himself a "disloyal" boy, and the act of writing about his parents "because there was no other way to fill the page" is painfully

36. "And he was waiting to be introduced" is written in hand above the first sentence. The more damning "had been told" is penciled above "remember." "Decisive" is written above the last part of the final sentence.

37. A pointed "finest" is written above this "better" as well.

guilt-inducing, as much so as if he had caused rifts and rivalries between living people.

So the version of "91 Revere Street" that finds its way into *Life Studies* from among various such manuscripts is in some ways a "whitewashed" account, and the whitewashing both alleviates Lowell's guilt over writing about such intimate material and makes space at center stage in the text for the father whose own powerful ambivalence, treated with a sense of guilty disloyalty by the son, assumes the central position in the story. The effect is also managed by the grandfather's removal: with him gone, the primary domestic scene is reduced to Mother, Father, and Bobby, the problematic nuclear family.

Shifting the weight of the characters as he had in "Beyond the Alps," Lowell puts his father figuratively in charge of the scene in "91 Revere Street." Ruling all as an opening trope of the opening passages is the ancestral portrait of the senior Lowell's dashing progenitors, identified variously in the manuscripts but called Major Mordecai Myers in the finished work. Thus "91 Revere Street" begins surprisingly auspiciously for the father, but the crucial ambivalence Lowell associates with this figure undermines the project. The ambivalence surfaces in the text itself. The admired ancestor is somehow "double-faced"; while he looks quite dashing, Myers's "exotic" eye seems to have "shunned the outrageous." In one version of the story, Lowell's father tells him that Myers was actually a civilian, and the boy abandons the ancestor as a role model, much as he seems to have abandoned his father for the exact same reason. In the published version of "91 Revere Street" this effect has been softened considerably, and Lowell conveys pity with his dismissal of his father's ancestor: "Poor sheepdog in wolf's clothing!" But when Lowell talks of his father's disappointing reality in contrast to pictures of the man in naval uniform and then brings in Mother "to insist to all new visitors" that Bobby's "real LOVE" is his toy soldiers, the child's willed distancing of the "double-faced" father is complete.[38] Any hope that Bobby Lowell will be able to take his father as a powerful role model has

38. Lowell, *Life Studies*, 12.

thus been stifled within the opening movements of "91 Revere Street," and the symbolic replacement of the father by a cartoonish "real" sailor at the end of "91 Revere Street" is hardly surprising.

Yet when Lowell presents himself as a young boy who prefers "toy soldiers," he is doing a version of what he claims the father does by putting an inexplicable distance between parent and child. That the figure of the father is so elusive in *Life Studies* perversely indicates that Lowell does identify with his father, albeit unwillingly, and that this identification may be the source of his ambiguous descriptions and his damning dismissals. The mother is made ambiguous only once in the *Life Studies* manuscripts, and this is a curiously failed list of linked traits: she loves both "luxury and Jung," her "heart was so much stronger than her brain," and "Her conscience and her lassitude were always simultaneously bawling for their pints of blood."[39] The list fails because the things compared aren't truly equal or even necessarily related, and hence can't provide the description of a truly paradoxical personality, in spite of Lowell's claim.

The figure of the mother with whom Lowell must be careful not to identify is generally described as both whole and forceful; she also makes Bobby feel impotent, and in this Bobby is surely the son of the man Lowell identifies as Bob in the manuscripts. Lowell makes the connection between his image of his father and male sexuality the thinly veiled subject of another passage from the "Rock" manuscripts. For the required masculine identification with the father to succeed, Lowell makes it clear once again that the powerfully whole figure of the mother has to be forcibly displaced: "If I looked straight ahead into Mother and saw nothing, I found I could imagine Father with a swan's feather cockade in his hat and leaning on his sheathed sword, more rash than wise among the Templars."[40]

The references to sword and cockade are unmistakably phallic, and by now the description of masculinity as successful soldiery is a recurring motif. The connection between success-

39. Lowell, "Miscellaneous worksheets," file 2230, Houghton Library.
40. Lowell, "Rock," file 2220, Houghton Library.

ful sexual identification and the father is made again, and even more overtly, in the autobiographical prose that identifies the mother as having "too powerful a spring." Like the man who looked at Greek statues until he forgot who the Greeks were, Lowell again offers a type of self-hypnosis as a coping mechanism: "One way to get around Mother was to think of the man's colors, blue and tan. Father's chair was leather and oak. The water in his two photographs of the Battleships New York and the Pennsy, was a gray that stood for blue. I was a tower of muscle rushing into air and water. Then I did my best to look straight ahead and into Mother without seeing her."[41]

Whatever the son does to displace the mother is a blow in favor of his own masculinity and therefore in favor of his identity. Bob stands in for Bobby in this regard, and if the father is portrayed as indecisive and fundamentally enigmatic, then the son, who is even less of a real soldier than the father, shares in the fundamental ambivalence of the male Lowell line. Consequently, the problems of the father are the problems of the son, an identification made again thematically in *Life Studies* when the persona becomes, at book's end, himself a problematic spouse and a "dim-bulb father."[42]

For the poet who tries to document his way back to artistic health through autobiographical prose, the dilemma remains wearyingly familiar, another version of the old problem of where to locate oneself in language, how to safely inhabit the center of one's work. In the Freudian scenario posed in the autobiographical prose, the unalloyed central power of the mother is both forbidden and dangerous to the identity, but the power of the father is enigmatic and so highly ambiguous that it is impotent. Siding necessarily with the father despite his own sympathies, Lowell presents himself as caught once again between nearly impossible alternatives—the owner of the same chronically dispossessed identity that held unwilling court in "Beyond the Alps."

While Lowell structures the autobiographical prose around

41. Ibid.
42. Lowell, *Life Studies*, 79.

the intensely Freudian conflicts of the nuclear family, the fundamental struggle is about the nature of identity in language, and it can be figured and refigured in any number of ways. This is to say that for Lowell, Mother and Father are invented characters in the autobiographical prose, fashioned by the self as a way of acting out the age-old question: Who am I? That they bear resemblances to the real people who were Robert Lowell's parents is unmistakable and widely attested to by friends and witnesses (especially in the case of Charlotte Lowell). But in no way should we read the story of the family as some sort of explanation. It is a familiar metaphor for the drama of the self, and, even more importantly, about the way a poet goads himself into writing that self. Lowell guiltily sets up his parents as opposite possibilities according to his usual pattern of the highly fixed and the highly free: one parent is immovable and disturbingly seductive, and one eludes the bonds of a fixed identity and is frustratingly elusive. They image the struggle within himself, the continual pull of warring voices that both engenders language and is finally unresolvable in form. No matter how guilty writing about the parents makes Lowell feel, the evidence that such writing provides a difficult rebirth of the self in language is often powerfully moving in the autobiographical prose. In one orphaned sentence Lowell enacts the first painful move back to identity through language by summoning together, for all their faults, the people who gave him birth the first time around: "I have nothing, nothing, nothing to say," Lowell writes, "my father my mother."[43] In this sentence he takes over the power of procreation for himself, transforming the pages' "nothing to say" into the names that long ago summoned forth his own troubled being.

If in the autobiographical prose Lowell makes the problem of his identity relentlessly Freudian, recent revisions of Freudian theory that describe its consequences for language match both the way Lowell talked about his writing and the way he actually worked. Lowell's dilemma in creating and revising the self also finds interesting corroboration in recent theory of auto-

43. Lowell, "At Payne Whitney," file 2227, Houghton Library.

biography. James Olney argues that autobiography has undergone a crucial shift from consideration of the "bios" to a consideration of the "autos." Since the self seems to be even less knowable than the life, autobiography has thus suffered a radical loosening from its already suspect moorings. The result is no fixed identity but rather "fictions of the self," as Michael Sprinker claims in "Fictions of the Self: The End of Autobiography," a primarily Lacanian reading of the situation that takes as one of its givens that "the subject is never sovereign in itself." Without the self as fixed and sovereign center, autobiographies become series of tried and discarded paradigms as the self struggles into a series of identities it can maintain only momentarily. As Paul John Eakin has argued about Malcolm X's autobiography, autobiographies operate on the "temporal fiction" of a completed self, and once the fiction is acknowledged, the act of composition "enters the life stream, and the fictive separation between life and life story, which is so convenient—even necessary—to the writing of autobiography, dissolves." The dream of the completed self lives on, Eakin argues in a wonderful analogy, much as the dream of producing gold drove centuries of alchemists. While the "pure ore of a final and irreducible selfhood" can never be achieved, the act of trying and discarding identities "in itself works to structure an apparently shapeless existence."[44]

Lowell's work in autobiographical material in the 1950s is a nearly seamless demonstration of such theories. For him the problem is always the creation of self in language, a process of division and loss. In structuring an identity poised between different possibilities, Lowell often posits dual choices: between male and female, between Mother and Father, between fixity and freedom, between prose and poetry. When he refuses to choose either side definitively, when he discards each possibility and then remains suspended uneasily between them, he

44. James Olney, "Autobiography and the Cultural Moment," 3–6; Michael Sprinker, "Fictions of the Self," 324; John Paul Eakin, "Malcolm X and the Limits of Autobiography," 192, 193. Katharine Wallingford delineates Lowell's attraction to Freud and the parallels with his own therapy in *Robert Lowell's Language of the Self*.

is caught in the autobiographical dilemma of the self that is fundamentally unknowable, which, as Sprinker sums up Lacan, "only emerges in an intersubjective discourse with the Other."[45] Lowell presses himself against his typically bifurcated others again and again in his work to let us see the radically different readings of his personality that each inspires. In Freudian terms, he tries to conspire with both the mother and the father. Each option, and of course we must acknowledge that the two options stand in for all the intermediate options as well, is finally alike in unacceptability because it would fix his identity in a way that simulates not life but death. The poet must always choose the indeterminate center because the shifting identities he discards one by one give him the only shaping he can hope to achieve in the fluid patterning of the time-bound world, in which fixed forms are waiting to trap us into something not our own. Even as Lowell seems to choose the father rather than the mother to identify with in his autobiographical prose, he takes the precaution of making the father in the most crucial ways unknowable. In other words, he is his father's son in this as well, and all attempts to achieve a pure and irreducible selfhood, what Eakin calls "the ultimate autobiographical dream," are doomed perforce to failure.

This is not to say that, bereft of usable patterns of identity, a psychological orphan, Lowell is powerless. By keeping his idenity suspended between power sources he cleverly situates himself in the vital middle ground, centered between acknowledgedly impossible alternatives. Lowell has thus constructed a way for his identity to be both center stage and irretrievably hidden in his work; he has made it into the type of unfindable talisman he longed for as a child. In the terms of autobiographical theory written nearly thirty years after *Life Studies*, he has taken the only possible position as teller of the story of the unknowable self.

If autobiography must, as such theories suggest, keep breaking down as the subject leaves behind paradigm after paradigm in search of a dream of completion, then it acts like lyric poetry,

45. Sprinker, "Fictions of the Self," 324.

which clusters around a series of non-narrative moments and works against the forward compulsion of the narrative line. I would argue that this is why Lowell's prose in "91 Revere Street" and in general is so luminously mysterious, and why it is so easy to break into poetry. As we have seen, Lowell's prose partakes of many habits recognizable even in his earlier *Life Studies* poems, before the death of the mother made the family story the most compelling formulation of the familiar dilemmas. His commitment to the divided and continually changing self is evident in the manuscripts not only in his characters and subject matter but also in his technique—in, for example, his unwillingness to provide straightforward syntactical referents, or clear-cut speakers for lines of dialogue. Such basic sabotage of his own professed choice thus undercuts every attempt to write prose "clearly, and in the style of a child." Autobiography itself always defeats such an undertaking, theorists of the genre argue. That Lowell's autobiographical prose acts not as the simple escape route he seems to intend but as a type of covert poetry, filled with trapdoors into associative depth and blank spaces in which words appear and struggle to connect over large spaces, suggests that Lowell was committed to the potential inherent in this particular method of division. Drawn to a clean narrative sweep of the past, he refuses to disable the flames and springs in his autobiographical prose. As a result we see as clearly as we do in his poetry the unhappy power of the divided self.

3

FROM PROSE TO POETRY

That Lowell's autobiographical prose presents a solitary, struggling self is partly a result of his method, partly the tendency of autobiography in general, and partly an acknowledgment of the fact that the poet's parents, those complex models of identity, are dead. The prose that discusses the parents' deaths (and the death of Charlotte Lowell's brother, Devereux Winslow) is grouped together in Lowell's *Life Studies* manuscripts as "At Payne Whitney." But despite the supposed efficacy of dealing with such events in prose, Lowell soon reworked this section into some startling new poems: "My Last Afternoon with Uncle Devereux Winslow," "Commander Lowell," "Terminal Days at Beverly Farms," "Father's Bedroom," "Sailing Home from Rapallo," and part of "During Fever."[1] Given Lowell's tendencies in revision, this reworking seems logical and even predictable in many ways. I have argued that one of Lowell's objects in writing prose rather than poetry was to avoid the painful depths of association poetry is prone to, to find a way back into literal and occupational health by following what Lowell himself seems to think of as a simple narrative line, a way of staying on the surface of experience and "rendering appearances." I have described the project as a failure in those terms because of Lowell's

1. Some of this material may be found in "Near the Unbalanced Aquarium," in *Collected Prose*, 346–63.

own deep-seated ambivalence, an almost pathological necessity to include everything and its opposite in his rendering of experience, acted out in the autobiographical prose by the conflicting pulls of Mother and Father. I also concluded in a discussion of the role of the self caught between these conflicting pulls that Lowell's autobiographical prose is organized around a shifting model of identity, and that this model is the prime dilemma of autobiography but the very bread and butter of lyric poetry. If, as I argue, Robert Lowell's autobiographical prose does act like poetry, nothing seems more natural than that Lowell should eventually break his prose along its natural fault lines into the form which is his most typical expression of the self. By rewriting his prose as poetry Robert Lowell also obliquely testifies to the effectiveness of his chosen form of occupational therapy: he is a poet whose inability to "think with my hands" has been cured.

The argument that Lowell's prose has been willfully constructed to work like poetry is rather unexpectedly bolstered by the fact that Lowell complained about writing prose as he complained about writing poetry, and in similar terms. When Lowell switched from writing a poetry draft of "Sailing Home from Rapallo" to imagining himself as Bobby Lowell in the autobiographical prose, he claims that "the labor, cynicism and maturity" of writing in meter were wearisome burdens. But prose has its own hardships: Lowell was later to tell A. Alvarez that the prose which became "91 Revere Street" "was an awful job to do. It took a long time and I think it could be less concentrated with more sting or something like that." Lowell told Frederick Seidel that while meter "plastered difficulties and mannerisms on what I was trying to say to such an extent that it hampered me," "it got awfully tedious working out transitions and putting in things that didn't seem very important but were necessary to the prose continuity." To both questioners he stressed that prose is hard to revise; working on smaller pieces, he can "work on it much more carefully, and make fast transitions."[2]

Such discussion implies that if meter "plasters" discourse

2. "Robert Lowell in Conversation with A. Alvarez," interview with A. Alvarez, 37; "Robert Lowell," interview with Frederick Seidel, 68–69.

with mannerisms and difficulties, so, in its own way, does prose. And prose has the drawback of being hard to rework, something Lowell was committed to as another defiance against entrapping forms. Poetry, for all the "smallness" of its "pieces," is not only more revisable but also more inclusive than prose: Lowell's newly airy lines in *Life Studies* seem hung about with any number of possibilities, just to one side of the "fast transitions." Prose continuity works against this inclusiveness by adhering to a narrative line; the very tendency Lowell once claimed to find freeing can take a stranglehold.

This restrictiveness recalls Lowell's complaint about meter, and Lowell takes his place uneasily as always somewhere between two uninviting options. His method in the bulk of *Life Studies* will be newly unmetered and less metaphoric and in these ways will be "prosier" poetry. Lowell offers further explanation for his seeming hesitation between these two problematic forms:

> But there's another point about this mysterious business of prose and poetry, form and content, and the reasons for breaking forms. I don't think there's any very satisfactory answer. I seesaw back and forth between something highly metrical and something highly free; there isn't any one way to write. But it seems to me we've gotten into a sort of Alexandrian age. Poets of my generation and particularly younger ones have gotten terribly proficient at these forms. They write a very musical, difficult poem with tremendous skill, perhaps there's never been such skill. Yet the writing seems divorced from culture somehow. It's become too much something specialized that can't handle much experience. It's become a craft, purely a craft, and there must be some breakthrough back into life. Prose is in many ways better off than poetry. It's quite hard to think of a young poet who has the vitality, say, of Salinger or Saul Bellow. Yet prose tends to be very diffuse. The novel is really a much more difficult form than it seems; few people have the wind to write anything that long. Even a short story demands almost poetic perfection. Yet on the whole prose is less cut off from life than poetry is. Now, some of this Alexandrian poetry is very brilliant, you would not have it changed at all. But I thought it was getting increasingly stifling. I couldn't get my experience into tight metrical forms.[3]

3. "Robert Lowell," interview with Frederick Seidel, 68–69.

Interestingly, Lowell makes no claim for himself as a prose writer in this passage, in which he vacillates nearly sentence by sentence between the disadvantages of different formal strategies for transcribing experience. In his judgment on prose Lowell speaks as a poet for whom the grass looks greener elsewhere, and yet he is convincing in his persuasion that somehow, some way, poetry needs a "breakthrough back into life." For him the breakthrough is accomplished, typically, by a principle of inclusiveness hard to practice and difficult to maintain: he will abandon his own "Alexandrian" polish for poetry that is uneasily freed yet seeks to take the life-giving qualities of prose to itself without prose's own constrictions.

Lowell's tendency to small pieces and quick transitions, not to mention his relentless organization of experience around a shifting, finally unknowable self, is steadfastly lyric, despite his championing attitude about prose. Furthermore, Lowell would probably have sabotaged every form he tried, no matter how long he lived with it, no matter how good he was at it, no matter how healthy it seemed to him or how well it suited him. "Breakthroughs to life" involve a kind of violence against whatever seeks to fix the self, which can be born only in separation from what one desires, in movement between possibilities, and in loss. Prose and poetry therefore have a characteristically odd conjunction in the *Life Studies* manuscripts, for they take on the same embattled duality of Paris and Rome, Mother and Father, fixed and free—of, in short, all the difficult pairings that represent and give birth to the divided self in *Life Studies.* It is characteristic of Lowell to try on the most extreme examples of these different possibilities. Ian Hamilton notes that when Lowell reworked his autobiographical prose into poetry he often tried to restructure first in couplets, an exercise Lowell himself talks about in regard to "Commander Lowell," an early draft of the poem about his father by the same name in *Life Studies.*[4] These poems in couplets seem particularly awkward; it is as if Lowell forced himself to make the most unlikely hybrid possi-

4. Hamilton, *Robert Lowell,* 262. Lowell's discussion of the issue appears in "Robert Lowell," interview with Frederick Seidel, 67.

ble of the formal options. When Lowell rewrote from the couplets, it is toward the unstable middle ground between forms and the looser, "prosier" style that was to become his trademark.[5] Lowell will use this newly won style, poised between forms, to construct a new identity in his work that will transform that work for the rest of his career.

As might be expected, when Lowell revises prose into poetry what he does with the figure of his mother is particularly illuminating. The prose from "At Payne Whitney" that is revised into "Sailing Home from Rapallo" is in the looser style from the earliest drafts; in fact, one version of the poem is almost literally broken into lines from the autobiographical prose, demonstrating the disposable nature of some of those aspects of prose Lowell found particularly annoying. A closer look at both prose and poetry versions of Lowell's trip to Italy to fetch his mother's body reveals that the poet's first problem was a general question of organization as prose becomes poetry: what to leave in, what to take out, and how to order the material he keeps in the poem that would become "Sailing Home from Rapallo." As usual, his decisions carry a full burden of psychological and technical implications.

In the initial, prose version of the story, Lowell takes us once again through the wreckage of an abandoned poem before he expands into the seemingly less painful prose method of talking about his mother's death.[6] This version is organized both scene by scene and chronologically, beginning with a view of Boston "on the nights when Mother was dying all alone at that little private hospital in Rapallo." Lowell describes the view as he sees it "on the road to the airport" from which he'll leave for Italy. The Boston setting calls forth other family recollections: passing the naval yard, Lowell is reminded of his father, and from that connection he thinks of New Hampshire, the family cemetery at Dunbarton, and his father's grave. In that last

5. At the time, Lowell maintained that couplets were actually closer to prose than were stanzas.

6. Lowell, "At Payne Whitney," file 2227, Houghton Library. One version of the story appears in *Collected Prose*, 348–50.

setting his father seems characteristically out of place "among some twenty-five Starks and Winslows." The scene, and his father's place in it, will be altered soon, Lowell implies. His father is unwelcome in the family plot "unless he produced a dead wife, a Winslow."

In the next section of the prose, Lowell produces the "dead wife"; he shifts the scene from the time his mother was dying (and from reminders of his father) to Rapallo the morning after Charlotte Lowell's death. What follows is a description of the hospital, "a firm and tropical scene from Cezanne." The scene is so beautifully described that the body at its center seems as artfully arranged as a centerpiece, and not exactly dead: "Mother lay looking through the blacks and tans and flashings from her window. Her face was too formed and fresh to seem asleep. There was a bruise the size of an earlobe over her right eye."[7]

The last detail is precise and artful and dangerously surreal: Mother seems to be lying with an earlobe over her eye, a description not restfully reminiscent of Cezanne but of a particularly disturbing Picasso portrait. Lowell ends the portrait of his seemingly undead mother (if her face is too formed and fresh to be "asleep," what is it?) on the particularly disturbing image of the bruise as if he knows that such associations are inherently dangerous. Switching into safer territory, he goes on to describe not the Oedipally forbidden body of the mother but the person of a vivid mother substitute, the nurse who attended Charlotte Lowell during her last illness.

In the prose version of the story, this nurse gives Lowell someone distinctly alive and powerful to be with while he confronts his mother's corpse. The nurse challenges death by looking "daggers at the body as if death were some sulky animal or child who only needed to be frightened." More importantly, she spreads around her own obvious vitality and brings Charlotte Lowell vividly to life in an account of the

7. Lowell amended "looking through" to "dappled by," making his mother less alive and more picturesque at one stroke.

4.

the verticals of a Riviera villa above the Mare Ligure. Mother lay looking through the blacks and greens and tans and flashings from her window. Her face was too formed and fresh to seem asleep. There was a bruise the size of an ear-lobe over her right eye. The nurse who had tended Mother during her ten days' dying, stood at the bed's head. She was a great gray woman and wore glasses whose diaphaneus blue frames were held together with a hair-pin. She had just pulled aside the sheet that covered Mother's face, with a flourish, and now looked daggers at the body, where death might have been, sulky animal or child that only needed to be frightened. We stood with tears running down our faces, and the nurse talked to me for an hour and a half in a patois that even Italians had difficulty in understanding. She was telling me everything she could remember about Mother. For ten minutes she might just as well have been imitating water breaking on the shore, then Mother was alive in the Italian words. I heard how Mother thought she was still at her hotel, and wanted to go walking, and said she was only suffering from a little indigestion, and wanted to open both French windows and thoroughy air her bedroom each morning while the bed was still unmade, and kept trying to heal the hemorrage in her brain by calling for her twenty little jars and bottles with their pink plastic covers, and always took her quick cold bath in the morning and her hot aromatic bath before dinner. She kept asking about Bob and Bobby."I have never been sick in my life." Nulla malettia mai! Nulla malettia mai! And the nurse went out, and said "Qua insieme per sempre, and closed the door, and left me in the room.

That afternoon I sat drinking a cinzano with Mother's doctor. He showed me a copy of Ezra Pound's Jefferson and/or Mussolini, which the author had personally signed with an ideogram, and the quotation, "Non... come bruti..."

FELT GUILTY BECAUSE SHE WASN'T ALLOWED TO TAKE

Prose that would eventually become "Sailing Home from Rapallo." Houghton Library, file 227, "At Payne Whitney."

American widow's last days. The nurse also performs a necessary function because she "had just pulled aside" the sheet covering Charlotte Lowell's face, a detail chronologically askew, as on the literal level of the text Lowell has already described

MOTHER'S DEATH AT RAPALLO
(February 14, 1953)

I

When I drove from Boston to the airport,
The needle of the Hancock Life Insurance Building
~~Was~~ flashing red storm lights
Through the brown tobacco spaces of night.
Angry, towering triangles of red lights, ~~sparkled~~ on and off.
~~Far to my left~~, below the super-highway overpasses,
The restored Constitution,
A black and white penguin,
~~Was~~ floating ready for action
In the Charlestown Navy Yard.
Midnight men were blazing with blow torches
On the orange side of a scrapped battleship.

II

I reached Rapallo an hour after Mother's death.
Her villa hospital,
Firm and Florida-like, ~~might have been a scene by Cezanne:~~
Sunlight rustled verticals of stucco
And watery, tufted pineti.
My Mother was mottled by black and green
Shadows from a blowing window.
Her face, too formed and fresh for a sleeper,
Had a bruise the size of an ear-lobe
Over her right eye.
~~Her~~ nurse for ~~her~~ last ten days
Stood at the bed's head—
A massive gray woman wearing
Glasses with diaphanous blue frames,
Held together by a hair-pin.
Lifting the sheet with a flourish,
~~She looked~~ daggers at Mother's body,
As if death there were a sulky animal,
Who only needed to be terrified.
The nurse talked to me for an hour in patois.
The sound was like pounding water.
Tears ran down both our faces--
Then Mother was alive in the Italian words--
All through her last week, ~~she thought she was in her Boston apartment~~
She thought ~~she was still in her Boston apartment;~~
Wanted ~~to open the French windows,~~
And air her bedroom from top to bottom
In the morning, while the bed was unmade;
Wanted to go out walking;
Tried to massauge away her brain-hemorrhage
By dabbing her temples with washes
From her arsenal of jars
With pink plastic covers.
"I was never sick in my life!"
"Nulla malettia mai!"

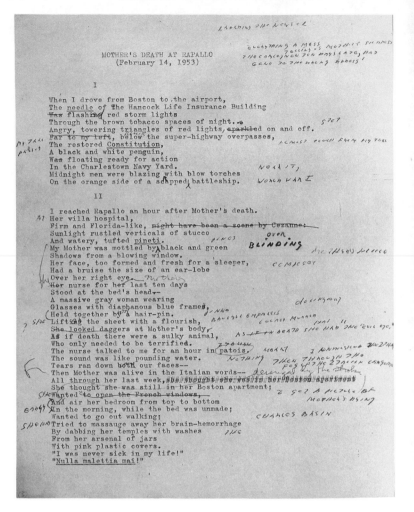

Draft of "Sailing Home from Rapallo." Houghton Library, file 2199, "Sailing Home from Rapallo."

the face before the nurse pulls back the sheet. It is as if without the counterweight of the nurse the portrait of Charlotte Lowell must stay self-consciously artful, weirdly distanced. Only when someone else is in the story with him can Lowell really bear to think of his mother as living, and hence subject to dying. He is pushed to this confrontation by the nurse, who figuratively as well as literally "pulls back the sheet" so that the grown-up son

2.

(Her young Italian doctor's
Presentation-copy of Pound's Cantos
Had the author's own felicitations:
"Non come bruti...")

III

On the Sunday we embarked,
The whole shoreline of the Golfo di Genova
Was breaking into fiery flower.
A crazy yellow and purple sea-sled,
Blasting like an unmuffled motor-bike,
Cut figure-eights across the bow
Of our little liner already doing twenty knots.
My Mother was sealed below
In a baroque black and gold casket,
Like the one in the Invalides.
~~We were now as solitary~~
Together as formerly,
When I took brisk boyhood walks with her
At Mattapoisett along the harbor
To the Ned's Point's Light-house
In September, the year's best season,
Unvexed by summer people.

In America now
Our family cemetery at Dunbarton
Lay under Mount Washington.
In sub-zero weather,
Its soil ~~was~~ changing to stone.
Its ~~black brook~~, its mast-smooth fir trunks,
Its iron spear-headed fence and its old-style memorial slates
Were turning blacker.
Father was there beneath his recent
Unacclimatized pink-veined ~~graves~~tone
With the Lowell motto:
Occasionem cognosce.-
Was ~~lying, where~~ the burning cold
Illuminated and gave a razor-edge
To the hewn inscriptions of ~~his in-laws~~,
Twenty or thirty Starks and Winslows.
Mother was voyaging ~~home with open arms~~,
And shining in her bridal tinfoil.

can come to terms with the fact of his mother's death.[8]

The nurse also seems to be a particularly potent figure because she speaks in Italian, a foreign tongue to teach a foreign concept. In the prose story of Lowell's journey to fetch his

8. "Beach, but" has been written over "shore, then." The change from "then" to "but" eliminates any lag in understanding: the mother is alive in the unintelligible language.

mother's body, the nurse's tale is at first beyond Lowell and, by implication, beyond everyone: the nurse "talked to me for an hour and a half in a patois that even Italians would have had difficulty in understanding." The language is so other that the breakthrough into understanding is a kind of magic: "For ten minutes she might just as well have been imitating water breaking on the beach, but Mother was alive in the Italian words." Lowell doesn't understand the nurse's speech, but by a kind of linguistic miracle he is able to "hear" all about his mother's last days: how his mother longed to go walking, to take baths, how she daubed at her forehead with tissues to erase the brain hemorrhage, how she asked for "Bob and Bobby." Charlotte Lowell has been translated back from death into life by the rhythm of a foreign tongue. At the end of the nurse's tale, Charlotte Lowell even speaks in Italian herself: "I have never been sick in my life (*Nulla malettia mai! Nulla malettia mai!*)." In the cry she is curiously vital and well at last, as if by dying she has been translated into another realm where such a statement could be not only conceivable but literally true. To the poet struggling to find a new style, such translation is linguistic power, and the final beneficiary is the mother's son. The man who can translate his dead mother into the foreign tongue of a story through the character of an Italian nurse has both reanimated the mother so that he can participate in her dying and achieved control over the strange hard fact of her death.

This done, Lowell closes the door on the scene: "And the nurse went out. *Qua insieme per sempre*. She closed the door, and left me in the room." The manuscript has been revised so that the Italian is Lowell's, not the nurse's, an act of appropriation identical to the persona's takeover of George Santayana's lines in "Beyond the Alps." In the prose story of his mother's death, the son has progressed from not understanding the foreign tongue to appropriating it for his own use, the revision implies. In so doing he has demonstrated his education in death, the most foreign tongue of all. The scene in which Lowell confronts the dead body alone, unlike the scene in which he seemed to be alone until the nurse "pulled aside the sheet," is absent from this version of the text. Conventional literary wisdom would suggest that the sheet has been pulled over the too painful confrontation. But Lowell has been careful to demonstrate in the preceding passage the process of his education in accommodating death. When the account ends, he has been armed for the meeting, and if words fail, as they do at the end of the paragraph, it seems to be because some resolution has been already reached and more rehabilitative talk is simply unnecessary.

To prove the point, Lowell moves the story forward in the next paragraph to "that afternoon." In this odd little passage Lowell sits "drinking a cinzano" with his mother's doctor, a gesture of male complicity. That the doctor takes time out from his day to have a drink with the visitor indicates that they have something to commemorate, or even to discreetly celebrate now that the mother is safely out of the scene, and that the two men discuss not Charlotte Lowell but the doctor's copy of "Ezra Pound's Jefferson and/or Mussolini" suggests that Lowell is somehow the doctor's equal, and, by implication, has an acquaintance with death as thorough as the doctor's acquaintance with literature.

But as in "Beyond the Alps," or the page of autobiographical prose in which he calls on Valéry and Freud before comparing his mother to Clytemnestra, Lowell's summoning of male alter egos indicates the imminent collapse of his own sense of control. Lowell's civilized grip on his mother's death is temporary, a fact indicated by the reintroduction of Lowell's father into the text. In the next paragraph Lowell begins to identify himself once again with that most ambivalent of figures: "And at the Italian funeral, I did everything that my Father could have desired." The first reading here is that Lowell could manage the funeral in a foreign place; the English arrangements he makes are appropriate to the status of newly arrived visitors, a description that fits both mother and son. Since the dead Charlotte Lowell had better luck fitting in in Italy than her husband had at overcoming the ancestral cold shoulder of the Winslows and Starks at the family cemetery, all seems to go well. But the son who is acting like his father now that his parents are dead gets into familiar difficulties when he sets out from the immediate small circle of Rapallo, where the influence of his mother still seems to work like a magic charm. The Lowell who seemed to have mastered the language in all senses of the word bargains in

Genoa for a casket appropriate for burial in Italy, though he would be taking the body back to America. Confusion immediately ensues, due in no small part to Lowell's own mysterious attitude. After crisply organizing events, he is at a loss when dealing with the casket, which of course suggests the corpse that will soon be contained within:

> Then I went to Genoa, and bought Mother a black and gold baroque casket that would have been suitable for burying her here, Napoleon at Les Invalides. It wasn't disrespect or even impatience that allowed me to permit the undertakers to take advantage of my faulty knowledge of Italian and Italian values and to overcharge me and to make an ugly and tasteless error. They mis-spelled Mother's name on her coffin as Lowel. While alive Mother had made a point of spelling out her name letter by letter for identification. I could almost hear her voice correcting the workmen. "I am Mrs. Robert Lowell of One Seventy Marlborough St. Boston. L, O, W, E, *double* L."[9]

Lowell, organizing everything "that my father could have desired," has begun to elide events in a way that has proved dangerous again and again by his own accounts. He has bought a casket appropriate for Italy to take back to America; his knowledge of Italian, triumphantly adequate for the nurse's tale, is revealed as "faulty"; and despite his mother's ghostly injunction to the workmen, the family identity has been skewed into a strange formation, the un-Bostonian "Lowel." (The mother herself seems complicitous in the transformation: by giving her husband's name prefaced by "Mrs.," she conflates her identity with that most ambiguous of figures.) The unlikely linkings in the prose passage of objects represented in the two countries and those countries' two languages has taken a dangerous turn. Once again such pairings indicate a radically divided self, and the initially exhilarating oppositions soon mutate into rather

9. In poetry drafts of "Sailing Home from Rapallo," Lowell hesitates between "Lowel" and "Lovel" before choosing the more exotic misspelling. Lowell often associates his mother with Napoleon, and claims that she instructed him "from the Napoleon book" ("Commander Lowell") when he was young. Napoleon is buried at *Les Invalides*, but the phrase also suggests both the mother's and son's hospital stays.

terrifying combinations. The son who heard the story of his mother's death, made arrangements, had a drink with the doctor, and made learned and civilized commentary has become the son who buys a casket as gaudy and useless as one of his father's cars, gets "overcharged" (the word suggests not only an inflated bill but the subtle rise of mania), watches his name, the word that speaks his identity, rewritten—and doesn't lift a finger to stop any of it.

In fact, the most intriguing suggestion the passage makes is that Lowell "permitted" all this: "It wasn't disrespect or even impatience that allowed me to permit the undertakers to take advantage. . . ." What did allow him is unnamed, but seems akin to the urge that compelled Lowell to strip the dingy adhesive tape marked with his name from the nail clippers at Payne-Whitney. It seems that in spite of, perhaps because of, his mother's insistence on the certitude of her identity the son must always question his, must once again dispense with the seductive idea of the unmovable central self. In permitting the wrong labeling of his mother's body, Lowell has managed to negotiate an obscure victory beyond the grave for his father, and consequently for himself. The mislabeling represents an escape hatch in the identity it represents; it momentarily frees Lowell from the domination of the name he has not created but received from his parents, and, therefore, from the parents themselves. In this last confrontation he stands down his formidable mother's voice; despite the risk to their mutual identity, he has done everything "that my father could have desired."

As if cued by the florid inappropriateness of the casket, the last paragraph of the prose account describes Lowell's festive leave-taking, when "the whole shoreline of the Golfo di Genova was breaking into fiery flower." The scene is theatrical: "a crazy Piedmontese Baron raced about us in a parti-colored sea-sled" (the "Baron" recalls Payne-Whitney's more colorful inmates). The scene seems an elaborate carnival in honor of the death ship, where Charlotte Lowell lies in the hold, "permanently sealed in her coffin." There is an oddly reassuring quality about the detail: "held" in the coffin as she is "held" in the ship, Charlotte Lowell is "solitary," and by inference her son is free of her at last. Of course, any such conclusion must be fraught with ambivalence, and it is worth remembering that Lowell always associates the central, unmoving position with Mother, and the position itself with a dangerously persuasive power. That she occupies the belly of the ship like the confiscated spring in Bobby Lowell's Christmas present may just go to show that despite the translation of her identity in death, Mother is still Mother.

Perhaps that is why Lowell's last, fanciful prediction of his parents' reunion finally rings false in this version of the story. "She shone in her bridal tinfoil, and hurried homeward with open arms to her husband lying under the White Mountains," Lowell concludes his story. His mastery of death's foreign tongue is faulty at the last, at least according to the testimony of that conclusion. The contrast between the invitation of "open arms" and the final solitude of "permanently sealed in her coffin" is too abrupt to be easily bridged, for one thing. The "bridal tinfoil," a term that fails to evoke much wedding imagery because it doesn't literally make sense, hardly distracts from Charlotte Lowell's deadness but accentuates it as we consider what "tinfoil" might mean in mortuary terms. Like the mad Baron's cavorting "sea-sled," Lowell's fairy-tale ending only makes us more aware of what occupies the death ship's hold.

Lowell's need to distance himself from the powerful mother holds true even in death, and the prose manuscripts of "Sailing Home from Rapallo" testify to his complex strategy for calibrating that distance. The poem Lowell fashions from this material for *Life Studies* is equally obsessed with this need.[10] The chronological order of the manuscripts is not clear, but it is evident that the version of the poem most closely aligned with the prose tries to incorporate the prose structure into its retelling and manages to transfer the underlying problems as well. In that version, Lowell takes whole lines from the prose and arranges them in sections identical to the chronology of the prose material. This version is called, most straightforwardly, "Mother's Death at Rapallo," and it is dated, interestingly, a year earlier

10. Lowell, "Sailing Home from Rapallo," file 2199, Houghton Library.

than Charlotte Lowell's actual death, a strategy Lowell also tried in poems about his father, as if moving the events back in historical time would provide a built-in psychological distance. "Mother's Death at Rapallo" is divided into a Boston section, a Rapallo section, and an "embarking" section in which the Italian leave-taking is juxtaposed with a view of the family cemetery, the latter scene representing the only change in the prose chronology. The poem moves in a neat loop away from and back to America, and while the circle's closure is anticipated rather than completed in the final lines ("Mother was voyaging home with open arms, / And shining in her bridal tinfoil"), a happy ending is predicted, with the couple, newly wedded in death, soon to be reunited.

Lowell immediately attacks the neat conclusion, revealing his familiar tendency to subvert any achievement of the supposed object of his desire. A reunion of parents would heal both psychically and geographically the rift between them, and it would also place them strategically before the wedding, and therefore before the birth of his own divided self. But as we might expect, the image is impossible to maintain, and Lowell revises it heavily by hand. He already seems to plan to include the misnamed casket in the last stanza, a move that would provide a forcefully weird antidote to the poem's neat structure and predicted upbeat conclusion. Lowell's tendency to disrupt the conclusiveness of this early draft (recall that Lowell had abandoned another version for the comforts of prose) takes other familiar forms. In revision Lowell consistently writes the other characters out of the story of his mother's death. The learned young doctor, that more expert alter ego, takes his Pound and disappears, though in several drafts he offers Lowell medication for "my hypomania," a detail that nakedly transfers the mother's brain sickness to the son, who takes the dead patient's place under her doctor's care.

With the loss of the doctor, who also carried the medication of masculine reinforcement into the poem, comes the near loss of the nurse, who is so vivid she obscures the other crucial female presence in the poem. In the *Life Studies* version, the nurse is in the poem just long enough to metaphorically pull back the sheet from Charlotte Lowell's final days:

> Your nurse could only speak Italian,
> but after twenty minutes I could imagine your final week
> and tears ran down my cheeks . . .[11]

After performing this linguistic miracle, the nurse discreetly withdraws from the poem, leaving the son to confront the mother's body alone. This confrontation, we might think, is the agenda of the revisions, and of the initial change from prose to poetry. Having worked through the difficult meeting in prose, Lowell is ready to face his mother in the poem taken from that prose. But Lowell cuts out that whole section in revision, as if the body of his mother has somehow escaped with the nurse, despite his assurances that he can now "see" the mother's "final week." Gone is the mother who dabbed her temples to blot out the hemorrhage, who longed in the prose for her daily baths and her constitutionals. Lowell switches to the embarkation scene, and the "fiery" flowering of the shoreline provides a fiercely ironic juxtaposition to his own reticence: in the space of the ellipses, the mother's body has been bundled into her casket unseen. Lowell has avoided sight of the corpse in the final drafts, and while he claims to see his mother living in his imagination we have only his word for it. Literally the poem's lost object, the living Charlotte Lowell never makes an appearance in the imaginative space of the poem.

One of the reasons for this crucial revision might be that when Lowell tried to write "Sailing Home from Rapallo" as a poem he found himself asking, in several drafts, an unbearably painful question. The living presence of the mother opens several versions of the poem with a query: "Has Bobby done anything bad?" In these versions the mother is "cuckoo from her stroke," but the question is a show-stopper from which these drafts never quite recover—after all, it implies that Bobby has somehow caused his mother's death. Such guilt, the suggested result of a childhood in which the son "wished we would all drop dead" and tried to keep himself from a fatal identification with Orestes, is immediately seen as inappropriate. In the poems in which it occurs, it opens the draft and then is imme-

11. Lowell, *Life Studies*, 77.

diately distanced by the mother's inability to judge (she is "cuckoo" after all) and counterweighted by other subjects and other stanzas. It may be judged inappropriate, but as a question from a by now truly "unanswerable motherhood" it is formidable and takes the first position in the drafts it inhabits. "Has Bobby done anything bad?" becomes the obstacle to overcome in this version of the story, and the nearly overwhelming guilt it suggests can hardly be therapeutic. When Lowell drops his living mother from the poem along with her doctor and reconstructs the nurse so that she is only a shadow of her formerly vibrant self, he does so as a gesture not of confrontation but of self-preservation. His solitude at the poem's end is sad but strategic: with the mother locked away in the hold, he can also repress the guilt he associates with her death.

Lowell's sense of complicity is nothing new, and it provides another reason for holding himself apart from those problematic sources of identity, the powerful parents. The poet who suggests in his autobiographical prose that he is somehow abusing his parents by creating them on the page is also vitally concerned that he has brought on their deaths. In two unpublished poems written between 1946 and 1951, Lowell treats the subject covertly.[12] These poems demonstrate their earliness in not having Bobby Lowell contemplate the dreadful deed himself but recruiting obviously assumed personae, a strategy discussed in the first chapter's analysis of "Beyond the Alps." In one of these early poems, initially called "Sailor in Fall River," but changed by hand to the more Freudian "Mother's Boy," Lowell imagines a "brother" who disobeys the mother by wearing an old bathing suit he had been forbidden to wear under his clothes.[13] This could be thought a minor defiance, but Lizzie Borden is a disturbing, nearly offhand reference in this poem, suggesting that such infractions are connected to larger crimes.

In another poem from the same file, Lowell expands his reference to the famous parent-killer. He takes on double personae, one of which is Lizzie Borden's sister, and describes this

12. Lowell, "Lizzie Borden's Sister," file 2179, Houghton Library.
13. Lowell describes a parallel incident from his own life in "Entering St. Mark's," file 2224, Houghton Library.

now aged woman's admiration of, and ultimate complicity with, her more famous sibling:

Lizzie Borden's Sister

"Lizzie Borden took an axe
And gave her Mother forty whacks;
When she saw what she had done,
She gave her Father forty-one."

Lizbeth and Calvin Coolidge were alive,
When we drove through Fall River on our way
Home from our place on Buzzard's Bay.
"Are you too tired to drive?"
Granny asked, and Father would explain
That overloading strained our Hudson's springs.
Old Annie, when she went ahead by train
To open house in Boston, noticed rings
Of gray and scarlet showing through my shirt—
A bathing suit that Granny meant to burn
Before she banished me to boarding school;
Would Annie tattle? We had made aturn
Into a private road of weedy dirt,
And Lizbeth, fat as Amy Lowell, sat
Grunting upon a lacquer stool
Before her goldfish pool,
And whipped a flyless leader at her hat,
A horse's hat that floated in the pool.

Night in our camphored house on Beacon Street:
O Granny, tell a story. Then I call:
Gran, you gave lying witness. "Ah, to fall
In Lizbeth's limelight, in the sheltered heat
Of Boston, by the capitol,
When judge and jury sweltered at her feet—
Poor impish Lizbeth, dressed to kill in black,
Displaying her seductive kgs and hands,
A girl and girlish. Could a sister lack
A sister's help? My friend, the parson, stands
Ready to lend a shoulder or an arm;
A former governor, Elias Stitch,
Orates into the tallow-oozing room,
As though at Groton on Commencement Day,
A parent to parents. "Come, come, come,"
He whispers, 'what's the harm?'

Besides Elizabeth had made me rich
Enough to marry as I wished.
Lizbeth loved Father, that's a truth: I say;
But I forget . . . I cleared her, anyway.[14]

This poem is very roundabout indeed, as "Lizbeth's" crime is only discussed in the childhood jingle that opens the poem, and the nature of "Granny's" defense of her more famous sister is quite unclear. The indirection is compounded by the fact that all this is cast as a story a grandmother tells her grandson, who has apparently disobeyed her by donning the forbidden bathing suit. But even expressed so obscurely, covert admiration for the killer of one's parents is a dangerous sentiment, and Lowell never published these troubled poems. However, the issue of bringing harm to one's parents recurs in the *Life Studies* material both in the autobiographical prose (especially in the brief, anguished list of associations leading Lowell to identification with Orestes) and in the drafts for "Sailing Home from Rapallo" in which the poet suspects with his stroke-damaged mother that he might have done something "bad."

These disturbing drafts suggest that Lowell knows that co-option by a desiring self is dangerous not only to that self, but to the powers-that-be he yearns toward. The potent sense of guilt that fuels these poems is also at work in "Sailing Home from Rapallo," demonstrating that if prose provides a "breakthrough to life," so does poetry, which plunges into the business of unconscionable associations feet first. Lowell is therefore misleading when he talks about narrative rapidity in prose and fails to mention the very different rapidity of poetry. Having maneuvered his way next to the painful subject of his mother's death in prose hasn't changed Lowell's dilemma psychologically or even technically, in spite of the fact that he's changed genres. What is changed in the poem version of the material is that he seems to know that he has to face his mother's death, as

14. Lowell has printed many changes in the margins, including the addition of the direct address "Boy" to parts of the Grandmother's speech, a revision which makes it clear that she is addressing the first stanza's child persona.

all else, alone; and to this end he assumes his own voice and writes the other living characters out of the poem.

This strategy puts Lowell alone on the deck of the ship carrying his mother's body, as alone as he is in the berth of the train hurtling toward Paris in "Beyond the Alps." While in "Beyond the Alps" his position recalls that of the mother in her casket, in "Sailing Home from Rapallo" his stance on the deck of the moving ship suggests that he has become a version of the seaman he remembers as his childhood father. In his shipboard position, too, he has assumed the father's rightful role and acquired the identity of "Bob Lowell." Now only the mother has the wrong name, and the son is implicated in the mistake he permitted to happen. The mother has been forcibly displaced from her identity by death, an action in which the son is complicitous. If the son has problems establishing his own identity as the ambivalent son of the ambivalent father, there is at least the guilty compensation that at least he is doing "all that his father wished." For all his bereftness, the son who sails home with his mother in the "hold" has, at least momentarily, restored the male Lowells to the manliness of "sea-duty" in the drafts of "Sailing Home from Rapallo."

That Lowell seems more alone in the poems than he does in the prose suggests that like all efforts in autobiography, prose offers only an illusion of continuity and community, a fact much clearer in lyric poetry, which has always depended on the lone, singing voice. When Lowell breaks his prose into poetry, he makes the natural fault lines visible by writing out many of the minor characters who people the prose. This effect is further achieved by his separation of different family members into their own poems. In one of the most notable examples, Lowell takes the prose description of his parents' house and puts parts of the house in different poems, as if he needed to put his subjects literally in their own rooms. The poem about Lowell's father's bedroom is particularly poignant in this regard. Lowell describes his dead father's room and it seems inviolable for the space of the poem, detached from the overflowing pink of Charlotte Lowell's spacious boudoir. The implication is that the father's room has achieved this status because the father no longer inhabits it, and the son who is alone in the poem with his father's belongings is for once free to contemplate the father's absence without the overbearing presence of the mother, with whom, he reports elsewhere, he often guiltily rehashed his father's failings while the parents were still alive.

Turning the prose to poetry therefore temporarily allows Lowell to separate out the characters of his life story, though they put in appearances in each other's poems. But despite this apparently desired result, the breaking of prose into poetry has the paradoxical effect of showing the connectedness between pieces. It is as if, having suppressed narrative connections, the poet has been freed to make the more mysterious connections that are the associative forte of poetry. These associations between Lowell's poems have been often commented upon, and the manuscripts offer new evidence that the reason the poems all seem to be part of one poem (as Lowell himself asserted) is that many had a common source in the autobiographical prose and, beyond that, in the same autobiography.[15] At the time he wrote the autobiographical prose that became the central poems of *Life Studies*, Lowell seemed to need to go the long way around to find himself alone on the deck of a moving ship. He unhooks the laborious formalities of his early poems in favor of the rapidity of prose and then dismantles that for poetry. Such movement across forms is the strategy of a writer who knows that what Eakin calls the "pure ore of a final and irreducible selfhood" is a prize beyond his grasp. Paradoxically, the act of trying and discarding identities in language itself works to structure his identity, so that even as the poet flees between forms, what we hear is an utterly recognizable lyric voice. To move the metaphor into young Miss Rodgers's art room, as Lowell ranges autobiographical particulars across more and more space, what we see is the image of one man's face.

15. Twenty years later Lowell insisted on the same principle when he dubbed the many sonnets of *Notebook* one "poem."

4

REWRITING THE FAMILY STORY

Son as Husband, Son as Father

In the winter of 1957–1958, Robert Lowell suffered another serious breakdown, this time after a respite of nearly four years. The poems written during the subsequent recovery period (Lowell was to be hospitalized again a scant year later) anchor the *Life Studies* volume, first published in 1959. Critics have rightly noted the frankly autobiographical nature of these last *Life Studies* poems. In them Lowell drops the pose of childhood and the psychological journey it implies and moves into the present tense of adult life. The person speaking the poems is not only grown up, but a grown-up who has lived with sickness: in each of the final poems, an illness named or implied forms one of the principal images. In "During Fever" father and child seem to share a mysterious malaise, "Waking in the Blue" takes place in a "house for the mentally ill," and "Home after Three Months Away" follows Lowell home from the hospital and describes him as "cured" while outside his building tulips quietly languish. "Memories of West Street and Lepke" and "Man and Wife" take on the language of the cure when they treat the "tranquilized Fifties" and describe characters "tamed by Miltown." In most of these poems, the illness is a lingering "enervation," but the husband of "To Speak of Woe That Is in Marriage" is on a manic upswing, "free-lancing out along the razor's edge." In perhaps the most famous example of illness in *Life Studies*, the persona in "Skunk Hour," whose "ill spirit sobs in my throat," proclaims emphatically, "My mind's not right."

While illness becomes a metaphor for the struggle to maintain one's identity in these later *Life Studies* poems (and Lowell is familiarly ambivalent about whether being ill or well is the more threatening), the old problems have been reworked in other ways as well. The family story that provides the most intricate paradigm of identity in *Life Studies* is, in the book's last poems, reworked for the poetry's present tense. Now the parents are dead—though Mother puts in strategic appearances—and Lowell himself has become a father. The transformation predicted by the manuscripts has thus been completed: the self who unwillingly identified with the elusive father has taken the place of that ambivalent figure in the family story of his poems.

The family dynamic has been interestingly reworked for the new poems, however. While Lowell has become a father, the wife of these later *Life Studies* poems is hardly Mother. The different weighting Lowell gives this new set of opposing characters can be seen in drafts of "Man and Wife" and "To Speak of Woe That Is in Marriage." Ian Hamilton has described the origin of these marriage poems in a single long poem: like much of *Life Studies*, they are related pieces broken down for additional polishing, and once again they serve to demonstrate Lowell's strategy of dividing up authoritative presences into different spaces so that he can confront them one by one.[1] Both poems are also obliquely related to earlier poems. Lowell originally seems to have identified what is just beyond "the razor's edge" in "Man and Wife" with a neighborhood whose otherness recalls the black youth in drafts of "Memories of West Street and Lepke." They evoke a longed-for vitality:

> Old campaigner, dear ideologist,
> The thirties single talent for seeing red
> Is nothing we can take to bed;
> You turned your back on me and kissed
> Your pillow to your hollows like a child.
> Our window was opened wide

1. Hamilton, *Robert Lowell*, 265.

> On the South End
> That razor's edge
> Of the Congo in the heart of Boston. Just like me,
> Refined past culture's possibility;
> At forty why pretend
> Others grow horny on alcohol, take the pledge,
> Free-lancing there along the razor's edge

Another draft makes the point more explicitly:

> On warm spring nights though, we can hear the outcry,
> If our windows are open wide,
> We can hear the South End,
> The Congo in the heart of Boston. Just like me,
> Refined past culture's possibility,
> The negro bucks
> Grow horny from alcohol, take the pledge,
> Fear homicide
> From drunken drivers,
> Free-lancing there along the razor's edge . . .
> At forty why pretend
> It's just the others, not ourselves, who die?

The "Negro bucks," sexually vital, aware of death, intensely living in the very "heart" of Boston, represent the allure of another self that is exotic, passionate, and connected to the business of life; in contrast, the couple in bed is not only less vital but seriously deluded for denying mortality. Or, more important, the wife is: the Lowell persona is fully aware of his flirtation with death, represented by a black counter-self "Just like me." In the earlier family story, Mother is a vivid presence whose failure is not in "heart," but in mind. But in these versions of "Man and Wife" the female counterweight to Lowell's persona is a thinker who has converted her ideology into a tirade against the ills of her marriage. She seems to be associated with head, not heart, and her husband finally accuses her of willfully repressing the sort of life-force he connects with "Congo couples," the phrase employed by yet another draft. In still another version, Lowell identifies this life force not only with the black Bostonians but with his infant daughter Harriet: it is her outcry that the couple leaves their window open to hear.

In some versions Lowell suggests that the problematic figure in the marriage bed isn't the wife at all, but the familiarly seductive mother.[2] In this reworking of the basic dynamic, Lowell's persona is no longer the secretly vital half of a marriage couple; rather, the couple is united in their instant effacement by the parent's vital presence:

> Eased by milltown we lay on Mother's bed;
> Even in darkness the yellow frame shone
> With the delighted abandon
> Of the morning I found her dead
> In Rapallo, a little bruise
> On her right temple seemed
> Only to point
> and not destroy
> The dogged overflowing wealth
> Of her still living health
> She could not lose
> While my mind grew unseemed
> And out of joint
> "I will no longer see things as a boy."

Lowell seems to have written this version next:

> Tamed by milltown we lay in Mother's bed;
> Even in darkness the yellow frame shone
> With the unchristian abandon
> Of that March day I found her dead
> In Rapallo . . . and though each plane
> From Boston to Milan
> Failed to connect
> And made me miss
> My mother's dying by an hour,
> She was alive. Outrageous power
> Rushed through the void
>
> Unhinge me and scream: "Young man
> Put on your toga virilis,
> You can no longer see things as a boy."

2. Lawrence Kramer argues that each of Lowell's "substitute interlocutors" is representative of his Oedipal sexuality ("Freud and the Skunks: Genre and

"Mother's bed" is a deathbed. But the mother's tenacious vivacity even in death is a version of the exotic vitality of the South End, where the inhabitants deny neither life nor death. This vitality is once again invested in an object that represents its owner's identity. The mother's bed is gilded with the unholy abandon of her death scene while the current inhabitants are drugged and untouching—they are the ones who seem most traditionally dead. The couple in the bed are thus strangely both matched and mismatched with this object over which they seem to have no ownership; the bed is another forbidden talisman of the sort Lowell's persona always yearns toward but cannot quite possess. The couple seems barred from the bed's "abandon" (and we remember that the mother has also "abandoned" the son by dying), but Lowell is his mother's son as well as his father's, and he offers a point of comparison between himself and his most powerful predecessor which suggests that the child has inherited at least one of his mother's traits. While his mother sports a "little bruise," it is he whose mind is "out of joint" or "unhinged," both terms also implying a relationship between two halves that has gone awry. In these versions of the poem he seems a sicker version of the vivaciously dead mother, and the wife implied by the poem's "we" is clearly no match for either of them.

The mother's presence in the marriage bed seems to have triggered this out-of-jointness, which has forced a change in her son's perceptual life. That he may "no longer see things as a boy," seems to indicate that the relationship between mother and son has ended with a perceptual awakening akin to a sexual one: with the powerful mother gone except for the talisman of "abandon" she leaves behind, the persona must acquire a new perceptual language. To put on the "toga virilis," the term for manhood written in a foreign tongue, implies that a certain potency is achieved in the process. But as always the revision of self into another form is dangerous, and the price may be an unhinging of one's identity from any possibility of a recognizably

---

Language in *Life Studies*," 83). I think that sexuality for Lowell is itself a metaphor and that he uses subtle variations in sexual "partners" to suggest various possibilities for recreating the self.

individual self. In any case, the scene holds little hope of marital happiness for the occupants of "Mother's bed," and in that feeling even the heavily revised poems in *Life Studies* concur.

The wife is perforce a shadowy character in these versions of the marriage poems: the son identifies their bed with his mother, not with her. In those drafts in which the mother is excluded, the wife's position is more powerful. She has, for example, her own "tirade," the section of a longer poem that eventually becomes "To Speak of Woe That Is in Marriage." But Lowell makes it clear that the husband and wife speak different languages and always have. She is outspoken, first person; he is third person, the omniscient and controlling voice despite the pleasing vigor of his wife's presence. Lowell makes the point even more forcibly by giving each voice its own poem: these people are two discourses, untouching as in the marriage bed.

Lowell's revisions suggest that by separating the poem into two poems with distinct voices and by writing out the characters of mother and daughter, he has used marriage as the vehicle for dramatizing anew the problem of the divided self that is at some level always a struggle between forms. He has controlled the story so that his character is mutable: he is both son and father, son and husband. In notable instances he has taken on the voice of both the mother and the wife, assuming their identities with their personae. As always in the *Life Studies* drafts, such powers offer both danger and a privileged position. The other characters in the domestic circle seem to group around Lowell's persona as warily, and as inevitably, as his own household did around the mother. The later *Life Studies* poems therefore suggest as surely as did the early "Beyond the Alps" that Lowell knows that the real subject in his poems is his own identity: it is the central story around which his poems uneasily group.

The newly central Lowell persona must elude some familiar traps, however. In the marriage poems the family triangle has been reworked so that Lowell's persona has in effect avoided marrying his mother, though the hapless couple is adrift in her furniture. The more interesting case is that of the parents' sole offspring. As in the previous version of the family story, a child fills the problematic but essential position of betweenness, and most intriguingly, this time around she is a girl.

Like Lowell's own bouts with mental illness, this birth is part of Lowell's autobiography: Harriet Winslow Lowell had been born to Lowell and Elizabeth Hardwick on January 4, 1957. At the time of her father's confinement in McLean's Sanitarium just outside Boston, she was a scant year old. In Harriet's character the problems of identity can be figured for once across gender, though it should be noted that Lowell had always written the occasional poem spoken by an assumed feminine persona. Marie de Medici in "The Banker's Daughter" and the beleaguered woman in "To Speak of Woe That Is in Marriage" are two examples from *Life Studies* alone. But the case of the child who turns the self into a father and simultaneously becomes a female version of that self is more complex, and puts a new wrinkle into old configurations of identity.

Harriet Lowell was born to parents in their forties, and from the first Lowell seems to have thought of her as a welcome revision in his life. As he wrote to his cousin Harriet Winslow before the birth of her namesake: "Two long cherished beliefs seem now to be failing me: 1. that children under five are unspeakable terrors, and 2. that children are engaged in an eternal struggle with their parents."[3]

The poet's ideas about children are surely linked to memories of his own childhood self. That he now hopes for something different indicates once again that he believes his experience can be reconstituted, this time in the form of a child who shares his name. The change in form itself is a signal for optimism; the same hopes he held out for the new strategy of prose writing are oddly echoed in his expectations that experience can be rewritten so that his child will not be an "unspeakable terror" (she will, in other words, have an identity in language), nor will she be engaged in the same power struggles that forged him.

To say as much means that while he hopes the child will revise his experience, he also hopes that she will not be like him. This puts an impossible burden on the child's own identity, and the way in which Lowell formulates his own desires in the case is typical: once again he arranges for various sides of a problem

3. Lowell, "Letters to Harriet Winslow," file 1641, Houghton Library.

to cancel each other out. The conflation of different identities into a functioning whole again seems impossible, perhaps because the authors of this new identity are, like his own parents, fatally flawed. Lowell seems acutely conscious that in one respect his child must not resemble her father. In an unpublished poem from this period, Lowell discusses a "stain" on the brain that, like his mother's cerebral hemorrhage, could be debilitating to his unborn child. These are its second and third stanzas:

So here in Boston twenty-five years afterwards
 I run the old groove again
 Along the Common and Public Garden
  Inkfish black in the brain
That cannot injure or stain our son or daughter
  Hung in its bag of water
  About to be born this season
Of births that must give quarter and quit
  For nineteen hundred fifty-seven.

Electric, suddenly oriental, a skeleton
  Blue tree was switched on the pond
 O Catholic symbol, plaintive toy
  I cannot look beyond,
How can this tree with its creche break new ground
  Or make my thinking sound
  Like a florescope
Picture of the spirit in the brain
  Of the child enacting our hope?[4]

Despite his assertions, the poet seems fearful that the "inkfish" *will* harm the unknown child, which is after all hung in water, a fish's natural home.[5] The spot in the brain that makes his thinking unsound must be countered by the "spirit in the brain" of "the child enacting our hope." Yet can this really happen? The poem's speaker seems to doubt it. The tree with its creche, which is the symbol of another birth, is a "plaintive toy," and the

4. Lowell, "Jaws jutting, eyes sunken in my brain . . .," file 2242, Houghton Library. The crucial *b* is scratched out of "brain" in the first stanza.

5. The phrase recalls Lowell's description of the "balanced" (or "unbalanced") "aquarium." The unborn child is also a desired object held momentarily in the center of its mother's being.

poem ends in a dubious question: how can this tree "break new ground" or "make my thinking sound"?

In this poem Lowell's persona seems to look at the imminent birth as a type of impossible salvation, and the problem, as always with Lowell, seems to be in his own conception of the divided nature of the self. Tellingly, the final lines of the poem can be read two ways: the picture of the spirit in the brain is his, within his own mind, and it can also be in the brain "of the child enacting our hope." If the unborn child already has "a spirit in the brain," then it can be for good or ill. There is no "florescope" picture to identify the life of the mind. She may, the suggestion is, have a version of her father's thinking, and therefore be subject to the same ills that have beset him—the "spirit" may turn out to be another inkfish.

The child of the poem also seems to be in danger because of the presence of the mother in the first stanza:

> Jaw jutting, eyes sunken in my brain—
>   No sophistication could cool
> My anger that would waste half
>   A vacation from boarding school
> Lugging second-hand lives of Napoleon
>   Across the Boston Common
>   Home to the stunned welcome
> Of my mother who dreaded my all-day browsing
> And dramatizing in my bedroom.

Indeed, the transition between the first and second stanzas makes it seem as if the baby will be Lowell's and his mother's; the second stanza's "our" seems to indicate the poem's obvious couple, set up in the unwholesome world of the opening stanza. This is of course forbidden territory, and the fact that the poet's mother also died of an unwell mind, a "bruise in the brain," makes the child's future as part of this lineage unpropitious at every turn.

The way Harriet Lowell appears in the drafts is itself instructive, for she is a product of revisions in "Home after Three Months Away," a poem that in its earliest form was less about "home" than about life in the sanitarium. Originally Lowell seems to have intended one long poem, "Homecoming After Three Months at McLean's Mental Hospital," which included material both from

"Home after Three Months Away" and what was to become "Waking in the Blue." The material about "home" may have been added to compensate, and provide a corrective, for the deletion of the Ann Adden material, sections of the poem in which Lowell had specifically addressed a "psychiatric fieldworker" from Bennington college with whom he had an affair in early 1958.[6] The sequence of revisions is unclear, but once the long poem that contains material from both "home" and "away" is divided into two shorter poems, the figure of the daughter acquires new stature. Over the course of revision, Harriet Lowell becomes a powerful female figure at the end of the title section of *Life Studies*, and drafts for this material show the poet working out the drama of the self all over again in his female progeny.

The long poem that seems to be one of Lowell's revisions away from the Ann Adden material includes parts of what would become "Waking in the Blue" and begins with the daughter's bathtub:

In my daughter's tub
The flesh colored rubber bear cub
Still dimpled with exaltation
Still with peach melba ears[7]

The scene's innocuousness is somewhat undermined by the implied absence of the daughter; the suggestion is that she has become conflated with her "flesh colored" bear cub, a reading supported by Lowell's past habit of referring to friends, family, and self as a network of bears, one of whom, "Arms-of-the-Law," is an ursine version of himself. More disturbingly, the poem quickly drops the domestic scene for the sanitarium, where the bathtub is no longer the domain of the daughter but of "Jimmy":

still hoarding the build of a boy in his twenties
as he soaked, a ramrod
with the muscle of a seal
in his long tub

6. Ian Hamilton has described this material thoroughly in *Robert Lowell* (244–46).

7. Lowell, "Home after three months away," file 2202, Houghton Library.

The distinction between the "cure" of "home" and the illness of "away" is blurred from the outset by the shared symbol of the bathtub, and the suggestion is that "home" and "away" are themselves dangerously mutable terms. The fact that in this early draft "home" is quickly subsumed by recollections of the mental hospital shows the relative strengths of the terms, and Jimmy's bathtub casts a vaguely troubling, vaguely sexual shadow back over the initial image of the child's bathtub.

After these first drafts, the McLean's material gets separated out. Once it does, the absent daughter takes shape, almost as if Lowell can introduce her more safely now that the powerful presence of the sanitarium has been put "away" in its own poem, a process which reminds us that Mother had to be stowed in the "hold" before the poet could appear on the deck in "Sailing Home from Rapallo." In one draft, he even calls the poem "My daughter," making her the shorter poem's subject and central character:

My daughter

In my daughter's tub,
the flesh-colred rubber bear cub
is still dimpled with exaltation;
its peach melba ears are as good as new.
My daughter wipes back a stringy lock
as I do. She tries to entertain
her poor relation.
Three months, three months!

Bushed by an April snow
and the second year's enervation,
our dozen tulip's flare
frizzled and small
muscle-wrung calves' tongues
lapping a coffin's length of soil
as black as cod liver oil.

For months
my madness gathered strength
to roll all sweetnes to a ball
in color tropical . . .
I am now frizzled, stale and small

In a more specific version of the dynamic of the original poem, in which the home is quickly overtaken by the sanitarium, this poem ends up dispersing into description of father rather than daughter, despite the title's promise. The ratio suggests that as Lowell is to his daughter, so the hospital is to home: each initial place or person is quickly subsumed by a more powerful version of itself. In "My daughter" Lowell arranges the material so that he is not really responsible for the takeover of his daughter's identity by his own. Here the daughter identifies with him rather than vice versa: she "wipes back a stringy lock as I do." Her identity seems to be compromised by her own wishes, and by her failure to adequately "entertain" her "poor relation." As a result, by the end of the poem she has vanished into the figure of the persona as surely as the child's bathtub is subsumed in "Jimmy's" "faintly urinous" "long tub."

The daughter is a stronger character in other versions, none of which put her in the title. In one version the poignant pleasure of having someone made in one's own image and likeness is clear, for in her one converses with a happier self:

> Three months, three months!
> Now Richard is himself again.
> Dimpled with exaltation,
> my daughter holds her levee in her tub
> Our noses rub,
> each of us pats a stringy lock of hair—
> our talking point is imitation.
> Oh nothing's gone.
> Though I am forty-one,
> not forty now, the time I put away
> was child's play. I can play,
> and say her name still. After thirteen weeks
> my child still dabs her cheeks
> to start me shaving . . . Once again
> my blankness starts to drain
> all meaning from this social strain . . .
> Dearest, I cannot loiter here
> in lather like a polar bear.

In this version the daughter, not the bear, is "dimpled with exaltation," a plump and confident version of the self who is correspondingly "frizzled, stale and small." Yet Lowell has often associated his madness with plumpness: in "Waking in the Blue" he is "200 pounds," another inmate is "roly poly," and in various prose drafts he has referred to the "yeasty" rise of mania. The "exaltation" of his daughter is oddly akin to this, and it gives her a weird ascendancy over the "frizzled" persona, despite the brevity of her appearance in the poem, and recalls the dangers associated with the identification of parent and child.

Despite this danger, the imitation of father and daughter is both mutual and functional: "Our noses rub / each of us pats a stringy lock of hair," and "Our talking point is imitation." The implication is that imitation provides a bridge from one form to another, and significantly, the link is a type of language. Imitation becomes a strategy for acquiring a new language and therefore a new identity, Lowell's purpose each time he reworks his material in a new form. It is worth remembering that the impulse goes beyond *Life Studies*. In his 1961 volume *Imitations*, for example, Lowell creates a "talking point" between himself and his predecessors by making his own language from other poets' work. The tactic has struck some as unpleasantly high-handed; critics were to quarrel over the ethics of both *Imitations* and Lowell's appropriation of language from his estranged wife's private correspondence in *The Dolphin*.

Yet this early draft of "Home after Three Months Away" seems to maintain that imitation is the preferred method of generating language: Harriet as preverbal baby proves the point. And in this version Lowell makes it clear that he needs to imitate more than he needs to be imitated. Under his daughter's influence, he can describe his time in the sanitarium as "child's play," as if the father has acquired a new context for his perceptions by emulating his daughter's activities.

While the acquisition of new language to describe his experience seems cheering, the effect is undercut by another type of "child's play" in the draft, one that reminds us of the danger of the whole undertaking. Lowell says, "I can play / and say her name still," as if the identity caught up in that name is as uncertain as the identity represented by the misspelled name in "Sailing Home from Rapallo." It also suggests that the poet is perfectly capable of toying with important names for his own purposes. The child's identity may thus be in jeopardy from the very person expected to safeguard it. Worse yet, he has written "at being father" in the margin, so that the revised line reads: "I can play at being father." The role itself is called into question by this revision, and the line also suggests that once again Lowell must play at being his father, the man who always seemed to be searching to remember young Bobby Lowell's name. Despite the exuberance of this draft's "dimpled" daughter, if Lowell wants to revise the father/child relationship this time around, the duplicity of his position indicates that the chances have already been undermined from within.

At this point in the draft, Harriet takes over, and in the second half of the poem the roles have been subtly revised so that now the father's identity, not the daughter's, seems in jeopardy. The daughter who "dabs her cheeks to start me shaving" demands that her father imitate her actions, and the result is a drain on his own stock of language:

> . . . After thirteen weeks
> my child still dabs her cheeks
> to start me shaving . . . Once again
> my blankness starts to drain
> all meaning from this social strain . . .
> Dearest, I cannot loiter here
> in lather like a polar bear.

This draft's daughter is strong enough to try to reconvert her father into the version of him she seems to need. Her command of their shared language finally triggers "blankness," a loss of "meaning" akin to a loss of identity. This must at all costs be resisted, even when, perhaps especially when, it is instigated by someone one loves, a "Dearest." This "draining" can lead to a takeover of one's identity: the fact that the father is "like a polar bear" at the end of the poem seems to indicate that he has become a bleaker version of the other drafts' "flesh-colored" bear cub. New versions of the self are desirable, but only when engineered by the poet himself; Lowell implies that his daughter has had too much power over his transformation. Her father just manages to slip away from being turned into a large and awkward version of his child's tub toy at the very end of the poem. He slips into a "blankness" that now seems more desirable than its alternative. The space at the end of the poem makes a covert argument against the unpalatable possibilities of the very language the poet wields.

The "blankness" image has been written out of the *Life Studies* version of this poem, and the revision indicates that once again Lowell wants to present himself as a writer cured of his stopped language, a writer whose "meaning," and therefore his identity, has been restored to him. The middle of the *Life Studies* poem offers no relief from the "social strain" of shared language, and therefore never threatens to elude its poet. It closes the escape route suggested by the image of lost language, and leaves its creator "cured," though nostalgic for the luxury of madness. Curiously, Lowell conflates this with a predicted nostalgia for his daughter: he will not "linger" in the bathroom any more than he will linger in the land of blankness, where control over his own identity, and over his power to create meaning, is at risk. In both versions of "Home after Three Months Away," the daughter seems to jeopardize her father's sense of self; her ability to both inspire discourse and draw her father into corresponding "blankness" is ultimately the threat, no matter how appealing, of a too powerful presence. In this, Harriet recalls her paternal grandmother, a connection not lost on Lowell. In a fragment at the bottom of a draft of "Man and Wife" he describes a couple virtually overpowered by their crying infant:

> Sweetheart, you tremble, tremble, tremble
> From across the bathroom baby Harriet screams
> Imperiously for our companionship
> Her jaw is like my Mother's in that photograph
> In Kansas City Mo.[8]

While the wife manages to evade identification with the mother, the daughter's identification with this powerful figure introduces new problems for the son-turned-father of the late

8. Lowell, "Man and Wife," file 2204, Houghton Library.

Life Studies poems. Lowell imaged the mother's strain on her son's identity in relentlessly Freudian terms, and in one draft of the poem that would become "Home after Three Months Away" the language describing the relationship between father and daughter is also sexually suggestive:

HOMECOMING FROM THE SANITARIUM

Three months, three months!
Now Richard is himself again.
Ruddy with exaltation,
my daughter holds her levee in the tub
he back is to the drain,
her feet on a dimpled rubber mat,
and she parts back a stringy plait
of hair as I do—all is endless imitation
She flirts, she flirts—
her honey-colored rubber bear cub,
a water pistole, squirts.

The suggested relationship between father and daughter is as psychologically dangerous as Lowell's "Waking from Mother" was in the prose draft of "Sailing Home From Rapallo." Such linguistic liaisons are Lowell's way of flirting with the dangerous possibilities of a divided self. Sexual metaphors are a traditional way of imaging separate but equal parts brought into fruitful conjunction, but by using the mother or the daughter as the other half of the identity Lowell seeks to join with, he has suggested the oldest taboo. Any desired healing combination cannot take place in this figurative formulation because at some basic level it is forbidden. In Lowell's case, he resists the combination because the resolution of division into one unified self is a longed for but dangerous illusion—an altitude, as in "Beyond the Alps," "we have no access to."

While Lowell seems to yearn toward the possibility of an undivided self in the family story in which he is the father, he subverts that longing by trying to set up his daughter, like his mother, as a version of his identity that is powerful and decidedly other. He does this in the *Life Studies* manuscripts as a way of keeping his child safe from himself and, more important, of keeping his identity under constant reconstruction within opposition. The poet/father therefore gives his daughter important positions in the drafts in which she appears: she opens the long poem about the sanitarium that is later divided into "Home after Three Months Away" and "Waking in the Blue," she is a vivid apparition in "Memories of West Street and Lepke," and the unhappy couple in drafts of the marriage poems hear her cry from their luckless bed as a moving symbol of their own unhappiness. Even her possessions are invested with residual power. In some versions of "For the Union Dead," the poem that originally closed *Life Studies* but later became the anchor poem for Lowell's next volume, Lowell takes another of her belongings and sets it up as a talisman to charm the poem into safety. In "Homecoming After Three Months . . .," the object that moored the poem briefly in domesticity was Harriet's bathtub; in drafts of "For the Union Dead," Lowell will try a similar ploy with her guinea pigs.

But even if Lowell images his daughter as outside his own identity—as female, vivacious, sexy and like his own mother—she is unmistakably his child, and therefore as incapable of resisting the power of the parents as he was. By this time son and father seem to be versions of the same identity in the *Life Studies* manuscripts, and if his daughter is fated to act like him, he is fated to treat her with something of his own father's bemusement. The "dim bulb father" of "During Fever" could easily describe both Bob and a grown-up Bobby. When a feverish Harriet appropriates her father's language by muttering "sorry" just as he does, she seems to be contaminated by the paternal identity, as if it were a disease in the gene pool.

Despite her power, the daughter is therefore ultimately unprotected from the encroachment of her father's identity in the poems she inhabits, and this is finally appropriate because she is the child of both his flesh and his language. For good or ill, once he creates her she is subject to an appropriation of her form for his own use. While this may seem like a violation of her identity akin to incest, Lowell instructs us that it is absolutely necessary for the self to recreate itself in new forms, and the borders of all living forms are permeable. Harriet may look like her grandmother and have a version of her intransigent presence in the poems, but for all that she demonstrates the ambivalence which is the heritage of being her father's daughter. In the last analysis she is ambiguous and unsafe, a small but colorful figure in the drafts, a version of the living self momentarily hooked in the flux of language.

Harriet also serves to demonstrate that gender is one of the first images of division, and Lowell uses her to experiment with the notion of sexuality as a mutable middle ground. If the poet's indomitable mother remains Napoleonic despite her vivid femaleness, infant Harriet undergoes a sex change in certain clothing: when "we dress her in sky-blue corduroy/ she changes to a boy," he claims in one version of "Home after Three Months Away." This ability to contain both sexual possibilities within the self is subject to the same ambiguities as are all oppositions within Lowell's work. Lowell's mother's manliness seems to add to her particular power, while Harriet's boy-ness make her more like her father and therefore more susceptible. The case seems to be different for Lowell's male forbears. Neither father nor grandfather are described as females; rather, the former seems something less than a powerful man and the latter something more.

Lowell makes an intriguing exception of himself, however. In an audacious act of appropriation across gender and taboo lines, Lowell speaks in the voice of his mother telling a family story in one unpublished poem from the *Life Studies* years.[9] This curious poem is a tribute to his mother's stature even in recollected girlhood, and having been a large and lonely child himself, Lowell creates a sympathetic if surreal picture of his mother's "alonehood" and awkward transformation. The poem deserves citing in its entirety because it offers the only example of the poet unabashedly assuming his mother's identity, though he often quotes her. In some versions he lets her tell the story, but in others he takes her voice as his own:

I was all back and shoulders as a girl:
Why? "Being," I would tell them, "just being
Makes me tired." And my brother and sister
Were always six years younger and more eastern,

9. Lowell, "The awning," file 2234, Houghton Library.

After my father quitted Kansas City,
The mine at Telluride to make us ladies
Seeing that he had made good, and came from people
As old as King Arhur, and predating Boston.
So my alonehood made me shrill, a little—
The way I used to put it was *I'm big*
As big as life and all out doors, a bus!
Oh hoping, hoping that some lovely no one
Papa, or just a noone, would descend
And cover up my eyes, and whisper, "Beauty,
You are a sober, usual size." But this
Is what I made of life. One afternoon
In Kansas City, I was in the cherry tree
Gobbling the cherries by the bucket-ful
As though I were a pheasant hen and starved.
My Aunt who'd studied under Liszt, my Aunt
The beauty, who'd turned down a Vanderbuilt
Or wouldn't let him ask, she looked and stammered
What, what, what, what!" My Brother and Sister said
"O it's a she-ape, or an elephant's
Ear flapping backward and white." My Aunt replied,
"But apes and elephants reside in zoos."
My Brother and my Sister laughed and said,
"O it's the hammock made from orange awnings
And blowing backward up the tree."
And then my Aunt, who took things as they came,
And was myopic, bored with children and a dear
My Aunt believed each word, and *awning* stuck.[10]

The mother is weirdly transformed into an "awning" by a type of family consensus at the end of the poem, after other namers have called her "she-ape," or "elephant's ear flapping backward." It is as if once Lowell takes on the mother's story she becomes subject to mutation, just as when he ordered her casket the family name ended up as "Lowel" or "Lovel." Such a reading suggests that for all the mother's seeming fixity as an identity, even she is not safe when she gets into the wrong cherry tree. The key to her transformation in the plot of this particular poem seems to be distance: when she is too far away to be seen clearly, her relatives can revise her identity. We

10. "Brain" is written in above "back" in the first line of the manuscript.

should recall that Lowell often employs similar strategies to create distance from the mother. The scene in the autobiographical prose in which he tricks himself into not seeing her by substituting the figure of his father is a clear parallel to the moment in this unpublished poem when the mother's girlhood self is suddenly transformed into an "awning." In the poem in which he takes on an experience his mother would have lived before he was born, Lowell uses his preferred rhetorical strategy to appropriate his mother's identity in language and, seemingly with the complicity of her own voice, convert her into something other than herself, merely a word that "stuck."

By assuming her voice Lowell seems to defuse his mother's power in these drafts, much as he manages to subvert all potent presences not directly imaged as himself. But when he uses gender as a description of the warring halves of his own being, the results are very disturbing to someone so caught up with imaging powerful maleness. In an unpublished poem included in the drafts of "Memories of West Street and Lepke," Lowell offers a series of striking descriptions of the self hopelessly divided across lines of both gender and race. "Death and the Maiden" (not to be confused with the very different poem of the same name in *Notebook*) is a powerful example of the anguish this particular brand of divided identity occasions:

Death and the Maiden

He sits beside me now and again
Waiting sentence in the bull pen—
The draft summons we still refuse—
A negro boy with curlicues

Of maharana in his hair . . .
Our short sentence was a year;
An extra day, though, was given
To make our trespass felony.

I am two people I confess.
One is this boy too hep to mess
With masochistic gallantries;
His bearing, all periphrasis,
Is single-angled to appear
Simple, sensuous and sincere,

And he glories in his stock
Allied with mine since Plymouth Rock.

He thinks his masculinity
Only created to be free
Of entangling alliances—
To turn all women's hands from his,
He swings a cane on which he's seared
Norwegian mountains he has cleared . . .
Its swagger caught my mother's eye,
My mother, in labor, wished to die.

Thank God my better self is woman:
All night she screams "*Nihil humanum*—
I'm alien to no alien thing;
The thousand thousand languishing,
Poisoned devils of conscience drouse
Outside my open floodgate house
And throbbing, glowing, reddened, whole,
We burn together, one live coal."

I squeeze my lifetime in this hour,
And yet there is no staying power;
My mind's spoiled rotten like a tooth,
When I leave the scarlet booth
Behind me to the rising sun;
My black self, the authentic one
Sits charring mountains on his cane,
His eyes, as blue as daylight, reign.

Shaving, I see myself as glass,
And laugh so hard I cut my face;
My black self, being stronger, twists
Under my skin with twitching wrists,
Mortal and cruel as Jean Cocteau's.
"Anything," it announces, "goes.
Time hangs heavy on your hands?
Buy me a pistol, I have hands."[11]

The suicidal shaving scene recalls the end of "Waking in the Blue," and it is linked to "Memories of West Street and Lepke"

11. Lowell, "Memories of West Street and Lepke," file 2203, Houghton Library. The line "The draft summons we still refuse—" in the first stanza is crossed out in the draft.

by marginal notes ("West Street" and "The West Street Jail") and the figure of the black man, awaiting sentence with Lowell. But while "Memories of West Street and Lepke" begins with a distancing frame (the persona is now as cured of his "seedtime" as he was of his madness in "Home after Three Months Away"), the "Death and the Maiden" draft shows the poet actively trying on the possibilities of a double identity: "I am two people I confess." This divided self has become the crime for which the poet must be sentenced, to which he "confesses," and that he identifies the two-sided self as partly black and partly female indicates once again that Lowell will choose radical and impossible options for a rebirth of the self. Both the woman and the black man seem exotically foreign to the depleted "Plymouth stock" the persona represents. Like Harriet, they represent a disturbingly exuberant life-force the persona seems to long for, and Lowell has no more qualms about trying out stereotyped portrayals of blackness and femaleness than he has about using a moron joke in another draft of "Memories of West Street and Lepke." Each figure is as unoriginal and as potent as Lowell's classically Freudian model of the family; they are commandeered to represent once again the self as unclaimed and untamable, less fixed than free.

As the questions of identity they raise are so primal, it seems appropriate that two important figures from Lowell's childhood make appearances in the poem. Lowell clearly associates both his grandfather and his mother with an impossible vitality of self imaged as robust male sexuality. In "Death and the Maiden" the black self's cane is an unpleasantly obvious phallic symbol; the cane is the notched Norwegian one Lowell identifies with his grandfather in the autobiographical prose. This super-masculine self is deluded about the power of his sexuality, however:

> He thinks his masculinity
> Only created to be free
> Of entangling alliances—

At this juncture a familiar entanglement proves him wrong—the figure of the mother, who is attracted to the "cane" and seems to get immediately pregnant. The sexual self is first deluded as a man and then punished as a woman: "My mother, in labor, wished to die." When the female voice takes over in the lurid atmosphere of the next stanza, the sexual imagery of fire, devils, and claims of remorse all seem obliquely connected to the mother who, Lowell claimed, did not want to bear her unborn son. At this point the poem seems to break down, as if the hard fact of that rejection, plainly spoken, is more than any formal constructs of identity in language can stand. The poem itself seems to go mad, coupling and uncoupling different aspects of the self. If at first the self was half black man, half female, the familiar Lowell persona now appears in opposition to the black self, "the authentic one," and to his own image in the mirror: he "sees himself as glass." In one reading, the poem's end is nearly desperate. The "locked razor" at the conclusion of "Waking in the Blue" is almost in sight and surely unlocked, as the black self "twists under my skin with twitching wrists." Lowell seems to avert danger at the very end by switching the metaphor: the twitching wrists seem to long for the razor that has already cut the face, but the black self asks for a pistol that hasn't even been bought yet, ignoring the method of violence to the self that is already close at hand.

While this poem clearly reflects Lowell's psychic distress about his identity, it also demonstrates once again his willingness to think of it as a writing problem, the same willingness that more quietly informs all of the *Life Studies* manuscripts. Switching names, even ones that seem most basic to identity because they identify gender, race, or even humanness, calling himself instead of "white" or "male" or "human" "black" or "woman" or even, in his mother's voice, "awning," Lowell makes his most radical attempts to subvert the fixity of form, revising toward what is finally an "unspeakable terror." Of course, this is an impossible task for a writer, and one that Lowell is chronically unable to complete, just as he is unable to resist the sabotage of every structure he employs. To refuse the momentary fixity of form is finally to give oneself over to a kind of linguistic chaos; for the poet who is writing his way back into health, the choice must always be to walk with some measure of formality the razor's edge. Even such a wild and tormented poem as "Death and the Maiden" recognizes this: the inclusion of a recognizable image of the self, the shape of the persona's face in the mirror, finally wrests the poem away from the near incomprehensibility of the middle section and away from the danger that threatens to annihilate the confessing double self. That and the confinement of the black self, who is by now contained within and relatively powerless (he has to ask for a gun), are ways of demonstrating a return to control Lowell exhibits even in this unpublished poem, in which, despite flirtation with a chaos of self and style, the final agenda is once again the solitary power of the poetic voice.

That control is even more prominently on display in the related poem from *Life Studies*. In "Memories of West Street and Lepke," Lowell is careful to set himself up once again as one whose "manic statement" is in the past, a man for whom sunrise has been converted into the small domestic vision of his daughter in "flame-flamingo infant's wear," the only reminder of the chaotic fire that consumed a stanza of "Death and the Maiden."[12] What remains in the *Life Studies* poem is a kind of nostalgia for the lurid visions before the self was "tranquilized" and, in an image he gives to alter-ego Lepke, "lobotomized." "Death and the Maiden" offers a chaotic vision of what it is like to live not with "lost connections" but with too many connections. The poet who consciously pulls away from them at the end of "Death and the Maiden" continues to rein in the possibilities of the self in "Memories of West Street and Lepke" because he needs to demonstrate that he is able, with regret, to make those connections between words and meanings that allow him to live in the world of form, no matter how diminished the remaining identity.

In this context, Harriet Lowell is a domesticated example of the dangers and possibilities of creating one's identity that are the anguished subject of "Death and the Maiden." Now that Lowell is an adult, situated at the powerful center of his own poems, both a husband and a father, he demonstrates a desire to stem the freedom of absolute fluidity of form for others' sakes

12. Lowell, *Life Studies*, 85–86.

as well as for his own. In the early *Life Studies* poems, Lowell expanded toward that freedom away from the powerful presences who had shaped him; in the later *Life Studies* poems, he reduces his stature and his possibilities in order to preserve others from himself. Both are finally impossible dreams: absolute freedom and absolute control are beyond the powers of any child, any parent, any spouse. And they are surely beyond any writer, of necessity caught between the fixed and the free, struggling to keep warring families of words from the "inkfish stain" that is a necessary condition of their birth.

Lowell works out his position through an imaged family once again in *Life Studies*. Having guiltily and regretfully negotiated to separate himself from mentors, parents, wife, and daughter, Lowell ends up alone in "Skunk Hour," though intimate domestic life is suggested by "our back steps." This aloneness is a strategic revision, however. In a related early poem dedicated to Elizabeth Bishop, Lowell's persona and his female companion (in one version they have a baby), are another obliquely troubled couple:

For Elizabeth Bishop

And we, we drove a car into the night
And climbed the tar's bald skull above the bay
To watch the moon whose mind is not quite right;
Nor was it hard to call her she and say
Her means and favors were miraculous;
Only God knew what she would do for us;
That's why I chose the sun and live by day.
And night, as usual, brought no thought to me;
Above the hedge of cedars stood the moon,
Lobotomized and full time majesty,
A stranger among us—that astonished one,
That downright one, too hurried in its search
For subjects, whitened deadly and royally
Above the chalk-white and pure spire of a Maine church.[13]

Lowell writes out his companion and disengages himself from the implied intimacy of parked cars under a full moon

13. Lowell, "Uncollected poems 1951–1959," file 2238, Houghton Library.

(what "Skunk Hour" will call "love cars") for the poem that will close *Life Studies*.[14] In the *Life Studies* version, Lowell has left such connections behind to become a community outsider, a conflation of the earlier draft's man and moon, and it is perhaps not coincidental that the wayward husband of "To Speak of Woe That Is in Marriage" is vindictively dubbed "Man-in-the-moon" by his wife in several drafts of that related poem. Both have acquired the status of troubled but privileged loners, and in early drafts of "Skunk Hour," the persona is explicitly made into the community's perceiving eye. "I am the visionary, the voyeur," reads one deleted line, neatly summoning up the possibilities of such an identity. As if matching the persona's solitary completeness, both mother and children have been rewritten in the *Life Studies* version to be beyond his power; they are safe from encroachment by a human identity and "will not scare."

Over the course of the *Life Studies* drafts, Lowell has demonstrated the need to appropriate the possibilities of language represented by other characters in his poems, but these skunks are not mentors he must dethrone, parents he must defuse, children he must protect, wives with whom he must speak but with whom shared language is impossible. With the arrival of the skunks in the poem, Mother's position in the landscape has been filled with something similarly forceful but even more resistant. What is the chance of learning this mother's language? Lowell treats the unaccustomed balking of his powers with wry humor, as if he understands that by "scaring" everybody else off he has left room for a peculiar joke on the self: the skunks are as tenacious about raiding someone else's territory as is the man who confronts them.

Of course, this is a sleight of hand on Lowell's part, no matter how convincing, or how real the psychic necessity that precipitated it. All versions of the self are a function of the language he generates, from Harriet Lowell in blue corduroys to the elegantly silly mother skunk and her children. All the powerful presences Lowell uses to goad himself into speech are ultimately names in a linguistic family that writers must shape to their own likenesses.

14. Lowell, *Life Studies*, 89–90.

While the poet seems to negotiate for his solitude by this method, there's no escaping the unexpected sense of connectedness his strategy incurs. In "Skunk Hour" Lowell goes the long way around to wrench his persona away from human entanglement, working his way through the drafts until he is not quite "right" but alone, in charge of a troubled landscape. Then he slyly rearranges the effect. With the arrival of the mother skunk and her children, the persona in "Skunk Hour" suddenly offers himself once again as a bemused male in a familiar family triangle, caught in a stand-off on his own back stoop.

When Lowell reworks his family story for the last *Life Studies* poems, he reenacts the dilemma of a self born in division, committed to the multiple possibilities of identity that division implies, working himself into positions he then undercuts as too fixed to be free. It is hardly surprising, then, that after the success of *Life Studies* Lowell enthusiastically tried to free himself from the powerful presence of that book, along with the autobiographical material and loosened style that remade his career. In an interview published two years after *Life Studies*, he claimed that his long streak of autobiographical poetry was at an end. When asked by Frederick Seidel if he would then go back to his pre–*Life Studies* "American version of heroic poetry," Lowell replied that at least he wanted the "freedom" of a more impersonal style:

> I don't think that a personal history can go on forever, unless you're Walt Whitman and have a way with you. I feel I've done enough personal poetry. That doesn't mean I won't do more of it, but I don't want to do more now. I feel I haven't gotten down all my experience, or perhaps even the most important part, but I've said all I really have much inspiration to say, and more would just dilute. So that you need something more impersonal, and other things being equal it's better to get your emotions out in a Macbeth than in a confession. Macbeth must have tons of Shakespeare in him. We don't know where, nothing in Shakespeare's life was remotely like Macbeth, yet he somehow gives the feeling of going to the core of Shakespeare. You have much more freedom that way than you do when you write an autobiographical poem.[15]

15. "Robert Lowell," interview with Frederick Seidel, 72.

After zealously working himself away from such tactics over the course of *Life Studies*, Lowell here makes a plea for the assumed persona, one of his own early poetic strategies. Typically, Lowell cites the example of a powerful male (and one crucially swayed by a powerful female) to sanction his preference. Yet despite this 1961 belief in the value of a "more impersonal" style, Lowell acknowledges that the subject matter of *Life Studies* is not yet exhausted; perhaps even "the most important part" remains unwritten.

Ten years after this interview, Lowell seems to have lost his weariness with autobiography; as he describes his career to Ian Hamilton, it sounds like a loop away from, and then back to, the preoccupations of the *Life Studies* years. In 1971, Lowell describes the continued revision of his style after *Life Studies*:

> After this, continuous autobiography was impossible. In *The Union Dead*, I modified the style of *Life Studies*—free verse stanzas, each poem on its own and more ornately organized. Then came metrical poems, more plated, far from conversation, metaphysical. My subjects were still mostly personal. In a third group, probably thinner, I wrote surrealism about my life. I also wrote one long public piece, the title poem of the *Union Dead*. My next book, *Near the Ocean*, starts as public. I had turned down an invitation to an Arts Festival at the White House because of Vietnam. This brought more publicity than all my poems and I felt miscast, felt burdened to write on the great theme, private, and almost 'global.'[16]

"Personal" and "impersonal," "private" and "global": the relation of such seeming oppositions is still on Lowell's mind years after he used "Mother" and "Father" to jolt him into language. They demonstrate his lifelong commitment to revising the self in his style, and the restlessness that kept him at it.

But by the latter part of his career Lowell is less anguished, or at least more accustomed to, the apparent contradictions of his method. In "Father's Album," a poem from *Notebook*, he applies the following principle (with the characteristic bravado of all his elisions) to his father, to Franklin Roosevelt, and to himself:

16. "A Conversation with Robert Lowell," interview with Ian Hamilton, 12.

"You learn to be yourself; at first it's freedom, / and then paralysis, then you are yourself."[17] While Lowell in this quote describes his familiar dilemma as a two-step tutorial, his work from *Life Studies* on demonstrates that the equation can be worked either way: from fixity to freedom, from freedom to "paralysis." What matters is the swing itself, the uneasy journeys between Rome and Paris, between Mother and Father, poetry and prose, male and female, husband and wife, parent and child.

In one of Lowell's most famous comments about *Life Studies*, he claimed that when he was finished with the book he was left "hanging on a question mark" and he didn't know whether the question mark was a "death-rope or a lifeline."[18] The metaphor is brilliantly simple and utterly characteristic: it dangles all the possibilities simultaneously right before our eyes. The poet's identity depends on a sign, a mark on the page that represents something, yet what it represents is a mystery: the sign is therefore both fixed and free. The poet who is "hanging" (like a sign himself) isn't sure whether the sign will be fatal or whether it will preserve his life: the terms "death-rope" and "lifeline" are deliberately matched in syntax, in syllable count, in rhythm. For Robert Lowell the opposite possibilities seem equally possible, equally impossible. The poet's task is to preserve this essential mystery for the sake of "yourself."

17. Lowell, *Notebook*, 132.
18. Stanley Kunitz, *A Kind of Order*, 154.

Bibliography

Axelrod, Steven Gould. *Robert Lowell: Life and Art*. Princeton: Princeton University Press, 1978.

Bell, Vereen. *Robert Lowell: Nihilist as Hero*. Cambridge: Harvard University Press, 1983.

Chandler, David E., ed. *Dictionary of the Napoleonic Wars*. New York: Macmillan, 1979.

de Man, Paul. "Autobiography as De-facement." *Modern Language Notes* 94 (December 1979): 920–22.

Doreski, William. *The Years of Our Friendship: Robert Lowell and Allen Tate*. Jackson: University Press of Mississippi, 1990.

Eakin, John Paul. "Malcolm X and the Limits of Autobiography." In *Autobiography: Essays Theoretical and Critical*, edited by James Olney, 181–93. Princeton: Princeton University Press, 1980.

Hamilton, Ian. *Robert Lowell: A Biography*. New York: Random House, 1982.

Irigaray, Luce. *Speculum of the Other Woman*. Ithaca, N.Y.: Cornell University Press, 1985.

Jay, Paul. *Being in the Text: Self-Representation from Wordsworth to Barthes*. Ithaca, N.Y.: Cornell University Press, 1984.

Kramer, Lawrence. "Freud and the Skunks: Genre and Language in *Life Studies*." In *Robert Lowell: Essays on the Poetry*, edited by Steven Gould Axelrod and Helen Deese, 80–98. Cambridge: Cambridge University Press, 1986.

Kunitz, Stanley. *A Kind of Order, a Kind of Folly*. Boston: Little, Brown, 1975.

Lacan, Jacques. *Feminine Sexuality: Jacques Lacan and the Ecole Freudienne*. Edited by Juliet Mitchell and Jacqueline Rose. New York: Norton, 1982.

Lowell, Robert. "Beyond the Alps." *Kenyon Review* 15 (1953): 399–400.

———. *Collected Prose*. Edited by Robert Giroux. New York: Farrar, Straus and Giroux, 1987.

———. "A Conversation with Robert Lowell." Interview by Ian Hamilton. *Review* 26 (Summer 1971): 10–29.

———. *Day by Day*. New York: Farrar, Straus and Giroux, 1975.

———. "Et in America Ego—the American Poet Robert Lowell Talks to the Novelist V. S. Naipaul about Art, Power, and the Dramatization of the Self." Interview by V. S. Naipaul. *Listener* 82 (September 4, 1969): 302–4.

———. *History*. New York: Farrar, Straus and Giroux, 1973.

———. *Life Studies and For the Union Dead*. New York: Farrar, Straus and Giroux, 1964.

———. *Notebook*. New York: Farrar, Straus and Giroux, 1970.

———. "Robert Lowell." Interview by Frederick Seidel. *Paris Review* 7 (Winter–Spring 1961): 56–95.

———. "Robert Lowell in Conversation with A. Alvarez." Interview by A. Alvarez. *Review* (August 8, 1963): 36–40.

Martin, Jay. "Grief and Nothingness: Loss and Mourning in Lowell's Poetry." In *Robert Lowell: Essays on the Poetry*, edited by Steven Gould Axelrod and Helen Deese, 26–50. Cambridge University Press, 1986.

Olney, James. "Autobiography and the Cultural Moment: A Thematic, Historical, and Bibliographic Introduction." In *Autobiography: Essays Theoretical and Critical*, edited by James Olney, 1–27. Princeton: Princeton University Press, 1980.

Silverman, Kaja. *The Subject of Semiotics*. New York: Oxford University Press.

Sprinker, Michael. "Fictions of the Self: The End of Autobiography." In *Autobiography: Essays Theoretical and Critical*, edited by James Olney, 321–42. Princeton: Princeton University Press, 1980.

Wallingford, Katharine. *Robert Lowell's Language of the Self*. Chapel Hill: University of North Carolina Press, 1988.

Williamson, Alan. *Pity the Monsters: The Political Vision of Robert Lowell*. New Haven, Conn.: Yale University Press, 1974.

Yenser, Stephen. *Circle to Circle: The Poetry of Robert Lowell*. Berkeley: University of California Press, 1975.

Index